1493

for young people

CHARLES C. MANN

ADAPTED BY REBECCA STEFOFF

1493

for young people

FROM COLUMBUS'S VOYAGE TO GLOBALIZATION

A TRIANGLE SQUARE BOOK FOR YOUNG READERS
PUBLISHED BY SEVEN STORIES PRESS

SEVEN STORIES PRESS
140 Watts Street
New York, NY 10013
www.sevenstories.com

College professors may order free examination copies
of Seven Stories Press titles.
To order, visit www.sevenstories.com/textbook
or send a fax on school letterhead to (212) 226-1411.

Book design by Pollen/Stewart Cauley/Abigail Miller, New York

Library of Congress Cataloging-in-Publication Data ,
Mann, Charles C.,
1493 for young people : from Columbus's voyage to globalization
Charles Mann; adapted by Rebecca Stefoff.
pages cm.
(For young people series)
ISBN 978-1-60980-630-9 (hardback)
ISBN 978-1-60980-663-7 (paperback)
1. History, Modern—Juvenile literature.
2. Economic history—Juvenile literature.
3. Commerce—History—Juvenile literature.
4. Agriculture—History—Juvenile literature.
5. Ecology—History—Juvenile literature.
6. Industrial revolution—Juvenile literature.
7. Slave trade—History—Juvenile literature.
8. America—Discovery and exploration—
Economic aspects—Juvenile literature.
9. America—Discovery and exploration—
Environmental aspects—Juvenile literature.
10. Columbus, Christopher—Influence—Juvenile literature.
11. Globalization—Juvenile literature.

I. Stefoff, Rebecca, 1951-II. Title.
III. Title: Fourteen ninety-three for young people.
IV. Title: Fourteen hundred ninety-three for young people.
D228.M35 2015
909.08—dc23
2014047241

Printed in China

9 8 7 6 5 4 3 2 1

Contents

ARCTIC CIRCLE

ANTARCTIC CIRCLE

Indian
Ocean

KOREA JAPAN

MING EMPIRE

KHANATE OF THE OIRATS

TIBET

CHAGATAI KHANATE

SOUTH ASIAN STATES

SHAYBANIDS

TIMURIDS

AK KOYUNLU

MUSCOVY

MAMLUKS

OTTOMAN EMPIRE

UMALWI

MOTAPA

DENMARK KALMAR HOLY ROMAN EMPIRE FRANCE SPAIN

LOANGO TYO

KONGO NDONGO

SCOTLAND IRELAND ENGLAND PORTUGAL

AL-MAGHRIB AL-AQSA

SONGHAY

Atlantic
Ocean

XINGÓ

Atlantic
Ocean

CARIBS

CARIBS

BENI

NOMADS

WENDAT ALGONKIAN ALLIANCES

HAUDENOSAUNEE

TAINO CHIEFDOMS

SOUTHWEST CADDO FARMERS CONFED.

MAYA

TAWANTINSUYU (INKA)

TARASCAN EMPIRE TRIPLE ALLIANCE

LATE MISSISSIPPIAN COMPLEX

~1493~

Pacific
Ocean

TROPIC OF CANCER

EQUATOR

TROPIC OF CAPRICORN

Introduction

ABOUT THIS BOOK

THIS BOOK IS ABOUT THE WHOLE WORLD, BUT IT began in a single garden.

More than twenty years ago I saw a news article about local college students who had grown a hundred different kinds of tomato. Visitors were welcome to take a look at their work. Because I like tomatoes, I decided to drop by with my eight-year-old son. When we arrived at the college greenhouse I was amazed. I'd never seen tomatoes in so many different sizes, shapes, and colors.

A student offered us samples. One alarmingly lumpy tomato was the color of an old brick, with a broad greenish-black patch around the stem. Its taste was so intense that it jolted my mouth awake. Its name, the student said, was Black from Tula. It was an "heirloom" tomato, an old variety. It had been developed in the nineteenth century in Ukraine, south of Russia.

(left)
Black from Tula and
Black Krim tomato
seedlings.

I

"I thought tomatoes came from Mexico," I said. "What are they doing breeding them in Ukraine?"

The student gave me a catalog of heirloom seeds for tomatoes, chile peppers, and beans (the kind of beans in chili, not green ones). All three crops originated in the Americas, but the catalog showed many varieties that came from overseas: Japanese tomatoes, Italian peppers, beans from the Congo. Wanting more of those strange but tasty tomatoes, I ordered some seeds, sprouted them in plastic containers, and stuck the seedlings in a garden, something I'd never done before.

My question to the student had been off the mark, as I discovered when I did some research. Tomatoes probably originated not in Mexico, but in the Andes Mountains of South America. Wild tomato species that still grow there are small, and only one is (barely) edible. The real mystery is not how tomatoes ended up in Ukraine or Japan but how the ancestors of today's tomato journeyed from South America to Mexico, where plant breeders made the fruits bigger, redder, and (most importantly) more edible. Why carry useless wild tomatoes for thousands of miles?

Why hadn't South Americans learned to use the tomato? How had people in Mexico gone about changing the plant to meet their needs?

These questions touched on a long-standing interest of mine: the original inhabitants of the Americas. As a reporter for the journal *Science*, I had spoken with researchers about new findings on the size and advanced development of long-ago native societies in the Americas. Eventually I wrote *1491*, a book about the history of the Americas before Christopher Columbus's arrival in 1492. The tomatoes in my garden carried a little of that history in their DNA.

After Columbus
My tomatoes also carried some of the history after Columbus. Beginning in the sixteenth century, Europeans took tomatoes around the world. After convincing themselves that the strange red blobs were not poisonous, farmers planted them from Africa to Asia. In a small way, the plant had a cultural impact everywhere it was sown. Sometimes the impact was not so small—it's almost impossible to imagine southern Italy without tomato sauce.

Still, I didn't grasp that transplants such as

tomatoes might have played a role beyond the dinner plate until I came across a paperback titled *Ecological Imperialism,* by a geographer and historian named Alfred Crosby. Wondering what the title could refer to, I picked up the book. The first sentence seemed to jump off the page: "European emigrants and their descendants are all over the place, which requires explanation."

Exactly. Most Africans live in Africa, most Asians in Asia, and most Native Americans in the Americas. People of European descent, though, are thick on the ground in distant realms such as Australia, the Americas, and southern Africa. They are successful transplants. But why? It is as much a puzzle as tomatoes in Ukraine.

Historians used to explain Europe's spread across the globe in terms of European superiority. They argued that Europeans simply had better social systems, science, ships, or weaponry than the cultures whose lands they conquered and colonized. Yet Crosby argued that, in the long run, Europe's most important advantage was biological. European ships that sailed from continent to continent carried not

(left)
Heirloom tomatoes, including Black from Tula at the top left and bottom right.

just people but plants and animals as well—
sometimes on purpose, sometimes accidentally.
After Columbus, ecosystems that had been
separate for ages suddenly met and mixed in a
process Crosby called the Columbian Exchange.
The exchange took corn (maize) to Africa,
sweet potatoes to East Asia, horses and apples
to the Americas, and rhubarb and eucalyptus to
Europe. It also swapped around many insects,
grasses, bacteria, and viruses.

The people who caused the Columbian
Exchange did not fully understand or control
what they were doing, but the exchange let
Europeans transform much of the world. They
turned the Americas, Asia, and, to a lesser
extent, Africa into ecological versions of Europe.
They created new landscapes that Europeans
could use comfortably—sometimes more
comfortably than the people who had originally
lived there. Crosby claimed that this ecological
transformation gave the British, Dutch, French,
Spanish, and Portuguese the edge they needed
to win their overseas empires.

Crosby's books helped give rise to a new
field of study: environmental history. Another
new field, Atlantic studies, looked at the many

important interactions among the cultures
that border the Atlantic Ocean. (The same
approach is being taken with the Pacific Ocean.)
Researchers in these fields have been putting
together a new picture of how our modern
interconnected civilization came into being.

Today we use the term *globalization* for
the growing web of connections between
economies and cultures around the planet.
Globalization got started when sixteenth-
century Europeans wanted to join the thriving
trade of Asia. That desire led to the voyages
of Columbus and others like him. By the
nineteenth century—almost instantly, in
biological terms—the economic trade system
had turned the globe into a single biological
system. Creating this system helped Europe
seize political power for several centuries,
which shaped today's world. Our ancestors did
not have the Internet, air travel, genetically
modified crops, or computerized international
stock exchanges. Still, when we read accounts
of how the world market was created, we hear
echoes of today's disputes about globalization,
which has brought both enormous economic
gains *and* ecological and social upheaval.

What happened after Columbus, new research says, was nothing less than the forming of a single new world from the collision of two old worlds—three, if you count Africa as separate from Eurasia. Columbus's voyage did not mark the discovery of a New World. It marked the creation of the new world in which we live now.

How that world was created is the subject of this book.

What This Book Is Not

Do not expect a complete survey of the roots of the modern "world system." That subject is too big for any single book. Some parts of the world I skip entirely. Some important events are barely mentioned. Instead, in this book, I concentrate on areas that seem to me to be especially important, well documented, and interesting. The story unfolds in five parts, with two chapters in each part.

Part One begins with Columbus and shows how his voyage, and other voyages that established trade between Europe and Asia, gave birth to a new era in the history of life. The biological world became united for the first time in hundreds of millions of years. The human world of trade, colonization, and resource use became united as well.

Parts Two and Three lay out the halves of the Columbian Exchange, the separate but linked exchanges across the Atlantic and Pacific Oceans. Part Two looks at the exchanges that developed across the Atlantic. The focus is on the first global craze for a new product and on the arrival of a new and deadly disease that helped shape African slavery in the Americas. Part Three shifts the focus to the Pacific, where the era of globalization began with massive shipments of silver from South America to China. Wealth was not the only thing transplanted to China, however. The ecological part of the Columbian Exchange altered the course of Chinese history.

Part Four shows the role of the Columbian Exchange in two revolutions: the Agricultural Revolution and the Industrial Revolution. Two plant species, each transplanted to new parts of the world, fueled these revolutions and helped the West emerge as a controlling power in the world.

In Part Five, I pick up a theme from Part Two and examine what in human terms was the most significant exchange of all: the slave trade.

This discussion focuses on how slavery worked and its later effects, rather than on the moral arguments against it. Today slavery is banned in every nation; readers don't need me to tell them that buying and selling human beings is wrong. Yet not many people today understand how widespread slavery was in the past or how many changes it created around the world.

Our new image of the past is of a busy, interconnected place driven by ecology and economics. It may be startling to people who, like me, were brought up on tales of heroic navigators, brilliant inventors, and empires won by technological or political superiority. Yet there is grandeur, too, in this view of the past. It reminds us that every place has played a part in the human story, and that all of us are embedded in the larger, complex progress of life on this planet.

Back to the Garden
As I write these words, it's a warm August day. Yesterday my family picked the first tomatoes from our garden—the garden that has replaced the tomato patch I planted after visiting that college greenhouse decades ago.

After I planted those first seeds from the catalog, it didn't take me long to discover why so many people love puttering in gardens. Messing around with the tomatoes felt like building a fort as a child. I was creating a refuge from the world and a place of my own in that world. Kneeling in the dirt, I was making a small landscape, one that had the comfortable, comforting timelessness of words like *home*.

To biologists this must seem like poppycock. My tomato patch has housed basil, eggplant, bell peppers, kale, chard, several types of lettuce and greens, and a few marigolds. None of these species originated within a thousand miles of my garden. Neither did the corn or tobacco grown on nearby farms. Equally alien are my neighbors' cows, horses, and barn cats. My garden is a biological record of past human wandering and exchange.

Ever since Columbus, the world has seen groups of people taking plants, animals, goods, and ideas from other groups and making them their own, adapting and twisting the new things to fit their own needs. Every place on the earth's surface, except possibly scraps of Antarctica, has been changed by this process. For five centuries now the crash and chaos of constant connection has been our home condition. My garden, with its parade of exotic plants, is a small example.

How did those tomatoes get to Ukraine anyway? This book represents, long after I first asked the question, my best efforts to find out.

—CCM

(right)
Heirloom tomatoes, including Black from Tula at the middle-right edge of the bowl.

Lines of stones mark the outlines of vanished buildings at La Isabela, where Christopher Columbus first tried to establish a permanent base in the Americas.

PART ONE

ONE WORLD

TWO HUNDRED FIFTY MILLION YEARS AGO THE world contained a single huge continent that scientists call Pangaea. Geological forces broke up this vast expanse. Eurasia and the Americas split apart, slicing the world into different ecological domains. Over time the two divided halves of Pangaea developed wildly different sets of plants and animals. The voyage of Christopher Columbus began to knit the pieces of Pangaea together again. The Columbian Exchange began with that voyage. To biologists, it is the most important event in the history of life on earth since the death of the dinosaurs.

The reconnecting of the world was a vast ecological upheaval with big effects on humankind. The Columbian Exchange underlies much of history like an invisible wave, sweeping along kings and queens, peasants and priests. This wave of ecological and economic change triggered by Columbus's voyage was one of the establishing events of the modern world.

CHAPTER I

TWO MONUMENTS

NOBODY ELSE WAS IN SIGHT. THE ONLY SOUND
was the crashing of waves as I stood on the
north shore of the great Caribbean island of
Hispaniola, in what is now the Dominican
Republic, looking at a scatter of rectangles laid
out by lines of stones on red soil. They were the
outlines of now-vanished buildings, revealed by
archaeologists. One of the buildings had slightly
more impressive walls than the others. Standing
like a sentry at its entrance was a sign: "Casa
Almirante," or "Admiral's House." It marked
the first American residence of Christopher
Columbus, Admiral of the Ocean Sea, the man

whom generations of schoolchildren learned to call the discoverer of the New World.

La Isabela is the name Columbus gave to that community, Spain's first attempt to plant a permanent base in the Americas. (Five hundred years earlier, the Vikings had established a village in what is now Canada, but it did not last.) Today La Isabela is almost forgotten. Columbus's fame is shadowed, too. These days he seems less admirable and less important than he did when I went to school. Critics say that he was a cruel, deluded man who stumbled upon the Americas by luck. Indeed, he was an agent of empire-building forces, and his arrival was a calamity for the original inhabitants of the Americas. Yet we should continue to remember the admiral. Of all the people who have ever walked the earth, Columbus is the only one who began a new era in the history of life.

La Isabela

Babies born on the day the admiral founded La Isabela, January 2, 1494, came into a world of barriers and separations. Direct trade and communication between Europe and East Asia were largely blocked by the Islamic nations in between. Africa south of the Sahara Desert had little contact with Europe and next to none with South or East Asia. The Eastern and Western Hemispheres were almost entirely ignorant of each other's existence.

By the time those babies had grandchildren, slaves from Africa mined silver in the Americas for sale to China, Spanish merchants waited impatiently for the latest shipments of silk and fine pottery from Asia to Mexico, Dutch sailors traded shells from the Indian Ocean for human beings on the Atlantic coast of Africa, and tobacco from the Caribbean had cast its spell over the wealthy and powerful in cities from Europe to the Philippines. Long-distance trade had taken place for thousands of years, but nothing like this worldwide exchange had existed before. No earlier trade networks had linked the world's two hemispheres, or operated on a scale large enough to shake up societies on both sides of the planet. Columbus began the era of globalization—the single, sometimes stormy exchange of goods and services that now includes the entire habitable world.

The king and queen of Spain had backed

Columbus's first voyage reluctantly. Travel across the oceans in those days was heart-stoppingly expensive and risky, like spaceflight today. Everything changed when Columbus returned from that first voyage in March of 1493, bearing golden ornaments, brilliantly colored parrots, and as many as ten captive Indians, all from the Caribbean—although Columbus believed he had found his way to Asia. Just six months later the enthusiastic king and queen sent Columbus on a second, much bigger expedition. Its goal was to create a permanent base for Spain, a headquarters for further exploration and trade.

Columbus landed on Hispaniola, thinking it was part of Asia, and founded La Isabela. Almost immediately the colonists ran short of food and, worse, water. Columbus had failed to inspect the water barrels he had ordered, and they leaked. Ignoring all complaints of hunger and thirst, the admiral ordered his men to clear and plant vegetable patches, build a fortress, and enclose the settlement within stone walls. Most of the new arrivals regarded these labors as a waste of time. They saw La Isabela as just a temporary base camp for the quest for riches, especially gold. Columbus himself was torn between

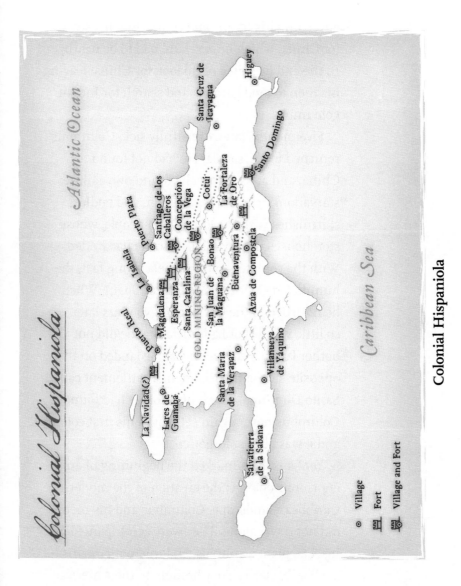

Colonial Hispaniola

governing his colony and continuing his search for China, which he was sure had to be nearby. In the end he sailed off to look for China, leaving his men to tend gardens and search for Indian gold mines.

Five months later, dreadfully sick, Columbus returned to La Isabela. He had not found China, and at La Isabela he found only failure: starvation, sickness, exhaustion, and endless skirmishes with the local Taino people, whose storehouses the Spanish colonists had raided. With the cemetery of La Isabela filling fast, the humiliated Columbus set off for Spain. When he returned to the Caribbean two years later, so little was left of La Isabela that he did not bother landing there. Instead he landed on the opposite side of the island, in a settlement called Santo Domingo, which his brother had founded. Columbus never again set foot in his first colony, and it was almost forgotten.

Yet La Isabela marked the beginning of an enormous change: the creation of the modern Caribbean landscape. Columbus and his men did not travel alone. They were accompanied by insects, plants, animals, and microorganisms such as bacteria. They brought to the Americas cattle, sheep, and horses, along with crops such as sugarcane (originally from New Guinea, in East Asia), wheat (from the Middle East), and bananas and coffee (from Africa). Earthworms, cockroaches, mosquitoes, honeybees, rats, African grasses—all these poured from Columbus's ships and those that followed, rushing like eager tourists into lands that had never seen anything like them before.

Natives and newcomers interacted in unexpected ways, creating biological bedlam. To take just one example, the Spanish colonists introduced the African plantain, a type of nonsweet banana that can be cooked and eaten, in 1516. At the same time, and without realizing it, they probably also imported African scale insects, small creatures that suck the juices from plant roots and stems. In Hispaniola the scale insects had no natural enemies. Their numbers must have exploded—scientists call this phenomenon ecological release. The spread of scale insects would have dismayed the island's European banana farmers but delighted one native species: a tropical fire ant. These ants discovered that they were fond of eating the sugary wastes of scale insects. A big increase in scale insects would have led to a big increase in fire ants.

All this is only an educated guess. Yet what happened in 1518 and 1519 is fact. In those years, according to a missionary priest who lived through them, Spanish plantations and orchards in Hispaniola were destroyed by fire ants "from the root up." It was "as though flames had fallen from the sky and burned them." The "infinite number of ants" swarmed through houses in Santo Domingo, stinging people and blackening roofs, covering floors in such numbers that people could sleep only by placing the legs of their beds in bowls of water. Overwhelmed and terrified, the Spaniards abandoned their homes to the insects, and Santo Domingo was "depopulated" for a time.

From the human perspective, the most dramatic effect of the Columbian Exchange was on the human species itself. No one knows how many people lived in Hispaniola when the Europeans arrived, although one careful study in 2003 pointed to a population of a few hundred thousand. No matter what the original number, the European impact was horrific. By 1514 only twenty-six thousand Taino remained.

Thirty-four years later, according to one scholarly Spanish resident, fewer than five hundred Taino were alive. The destruction of the Taino plunged Santo Domingo into poverty because the colonists had wiped out their own labor force.

Spanish cruelty played its part in the disaster, but a larger cause was the Columbian Exchange. Before Columbus, the Americas had none of the epidemic diseases that were common in Europe and Asia. The viruses that cause smallpox, influenza, hepatitis, measles, and viral pneumonia were unknown. So were the bacteria that cause tuberculosis, diphtheria, cholera, and typhus. Shipped across the ocean from Europe, these diseases and others consumed the population of Hispaniola with stunning fierceness. Throughout the sixteenth and seventeenth centuries new microorganisms spread across the Americas, ricocheting from victim to victim, killing three-quarters or more of the people in the hemisphere. It was as if the suffering that these diseases had caused in Eurasia over thousands of years were concentrated into decades in the Americas. In all of human history there is no population catastrophe like it.

WHAT KILLED COLUMBUS?

BECAUSE THE EXPEDITION AT LA ISABELA WAS desperately short of water, the men drank from rivers. Some researchers believe that this caused Columbus and his men to catch shigellosis, a disease caused by a bacterium that is native to the American tropics.

The shigellosis bacterium is carried in feces, the solid waste of animals and humans. It can enter new hosts through contaminated water. People infected by the bacterium can develop Reiter's syndrome, a disease of the autoimmune system. Sufferers from Reiter's syndrome feel as if large chunks of their bodies, including their eyes and bowels, are swollen and inflamed. Columbus endured severe attacks of these symptoms a few

months after arriving at La Isabela. His writings reveal that the suffering continued on and off for years, with painful episodes that left him unable to see or walk, sometimes bleeding from the eyes. "Most people don't realize that Columbus died a crippled man," says Dr. Frank Arnett, an expert on Reiter's syndrome, which is also called reactive arthritis. "He was bedridden. He was in so much pain he couldn't write or stand. He was very sick."

Reiter's syndrome is always painful and sometimes fatal. If it led to the admiral's death years later at the age of fifty-four, as some scientists believe, and if the cause of the syndrome was shigellosis infection, Columbus himself was one of the first victims of the Columbian Exchange.

Christopher Columbus on his death bed, as imagined by an artist in 1893.

To the Lighthouse

A peaceful, whispering river runs through Santo Domingo, capital of the Dominican Republic. On the west bank stands the stony remains of the colonial town, including the palace of Christopher Columbus's first-born son, Diego. From the east bank rises a vast hill of stained concrete laid out in the shape of a giant cross and topped with lights pointing to the heavens. It is the Columbus Lighthouse, completed in 1992 as a memorial to the admiral.

The idea of a grand memorial to Columbus was raised in 1852, but it took almost a century and a half for the memorial to be built. In that time and up until today, ideas about Columbus changed. From being seen as a heroic explorer, a leader, and a messenger bringing God's word to the Americas, he has come to be viewed by many as brutal, greedy, fanatical, and incompetent. Should there be any monument to his voyages at all? The answer is hard to arrive at, even though his life is one of the best documented of his time.

During his life, nobody knew him as Columbus. He was baptized Cristoforo Colombo by his Italian family, but after moving to Spain in 1483 he called himself Cristóbal

Colón. His thoughts were dominated by towering personal ambition and profound religious faith. Perhaps ashamed of his humble origins, he spent his entire adult life trying to establish a dynasty that would be given noble status by a monarch. He believed that if Spain could establish trade with China, the resulting wealth would allow the Spanish rulers to conquer the biblical Holy Land of the Middle East, which had come under Islamic control. Columbus wanted to be the one to begin that trade by finding a sea route to China.

Central to Columbus's scheme were his views on the size and shape of the world. Generations of schoolchildren were taught that, before Columbus, the people of Europe thought the world was flat. Nothing could be further from the truth. Scholars had known for fifteen hundred years that the world was large and round. Columbus disputed both facts. He argued that the world was not round but pear shaped. This mattered less than its size—and there Columbus was badly off the mark. He believed the distance around the planet was about five thousand miles less than it actually is.

Columbus's vision enticed the Spanish

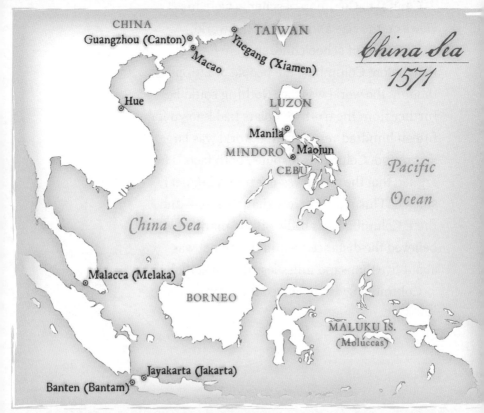

China Sea
1571

CHINA
Guangzhou (Canton)
Macao
Yuegang (Xiamen)
TAIWAN

Hue

LUZON

Manila
MINDORO · Maojun
CEBU

China Sea

Pacific

Ocean

Malacca (Melaka)

BORNEO

MALUKU IS.
(Moluccas)

Jayakarta (Jakarta)

Banten (Bantam)

monarchs. Like other wealthy and powerful Europeans, they were fascinated by accounts of the richness and sophistication of China. They lusted after Asian silks, gems, spices, and the fine pottery known as porcelain. Yet merchants and governments associated with Islam—people with whom Christian Europe had been at war for centuries—stood in the way of overland trade between Europe and China. Worse, the trading cities of Venice and Genoa, in Italy, had already cut a deal with Islamic forces and now controlled the Asia trade. To cut out these unwanted middlemen, Portugal had been trying to send ships all the way around Africa—a long, risky, and expensive journey. Columbus told the rulers of Spain that there was an easier way: west, across the Atlantic. He expected to reach the east coast of China by sailing west across the Atlantic Ocean from Europe. Unfortunately for his plan, not only did he greatly underestimate the distance, but he did not know that the American continents and the Pacific Ocean lay in his way.

After landing in the Americas in 1492, the admiral naturally claimed that his ideas had been proven true, and that he had reached Asia. The delighted monarchs awarded him honors

(*top left*)
This huge, cross-shaped memorial to Columbus in Santo Domingo was designed in 1931 by the young Scottish architect Joseph Lea Gleave, who tried to capture in stone what he thought was Columbus's most important role: the one who carried Christianity to the Americas. Political controversies delayed its construction for six decades.

(*bottom left*)
Map: China Sea, 1571

and wealth. Columbus died in 1506, a rich man surrounded by a loving family—but nevertheless bitter, and not just because of his illnesses. His personal and geographical failings had caused the Spanish court to take away most of his privileges and push him to the sidelines.

Much the same mixture of high hopes and disappointment is true of the Columbus Lighthouse. Although the nations of the Western Hemisphere had agreed in 1923 to build a memorial to the admiral, it was six decades before it was constructed. During that time, international support for the monument faded, partly because the Dominican Republic was ruled for years by a tyrant named Rafael Trujillo. His reign was barbarous, and supporting the lighthouse project was seen as supporting the dictator. Many nations boycotted the opening of the monument. Protesters set fire to police barricades, calling Columbus "the exterminator of a race." People living in the walled-off slums around the monument told reporters that Columbus deserved no recognition at all.

Their belief is understandable but mistaken. Because of the far-reaching effects of the Columbian Exchange that began with his voyages, Columbus's journeys marked the beginning of a new biological era in which places that were once ecologically distinct have become more alike. In this sense the once-separate parts of the world have been tied together, exactly as the old admiral hoped. The lighthouse in Santo Domingo should be seen less as a celebration of the man than as a recognition of the world he almost accidentally created—the world we live in today.

Statues in Manila

The island nation of the Philippines lies in the western Pacific, south of Japan. In a park in its capital city of Manila stands a marble pillar topped by life-size statues of two men. One man carries a cross, the other a sword. Compared to the Columbus Lighthouse in Santo Domingo, this monument is small and rarely visited by tourists. Yet it is the closest thing the world has to an official recognition of the origins of globalization.

The man with the sword is Miguel López de Legazpi, the founder of modern Manila. The man with the cross is Andrés Ochoa de Urdaneta y Cerain, the navigator who guided Legazpi's five Spanish ships across the Pacific to

Miguel López de Legazpi and Andrés de Urdaneta began the silver trade across the Pacific Ocean. This statue in a park in Manila is as close to a monument to globalization as the world is likely to see.

the Philippines from Spain's colony in Mexico in 1564. Together these friends and cousins achieved what Columbus failed to do. They established trade with China by sailing west. They launched the economic unification of the world, just as Columbus launched its ecological unification.

Urdaneta's second achievement was figuring out how to sail back to Mexico. He could not simply retrace the route the expedition had followed to the Philippines, because the trade winds that had blown the ships westward would block their return. In a stroke of navigational genius, Urdaneta avoided the currents by sailing far north before turning east. In this way he established a route that ships would follow for years to come.

Meanwhile, plagued by mutiny and disease, and harassed by ships from Spain's rival Portugal, Legazpi slowly spread Spanish influence in the Philippine islands. Eventually some of his men made contact with two trading junks, ships that had come from China to exchange porcelain, silk, perfumes, and other goods for Philippine gold and beeswax. The Chinese returned to their homeland with word that Europeans had arrived in the Philippines. Amazingly, they had come from east of China, although Europe lay to the west. Furthermore, the European "barbarians" had something that was extremely desirable in China: silver. Two years later, three junks from China appeared in the Philippines loaded with silks, porcelain, and other goods to trade at Legazpi's outpost in Manila. In return, the Chinese took every ounce of Spanish silver.

More junks came the next year, and the year after that. Driven by China's hunger for silver and Europe's hunger for silk and porcelain, the trade grew enormous. The "galleon trade," as it was called after the large ships known as galleons, linked Asia, Europe, and Africa, the source of the slaves who dug the silver out of Mexico's mines. Never before had so much of the planet been linked in a single network of exchange. With Spain's arrival in the Philippines, a new, distinctly modern era had dawned.

The new era was regarded with suspicion from the start. China was then the world's wealthiest, most powerful nation. It had long viewed Europe as too poor and backward to be of commercial interest. When Spain discovered huge amounts of silver in South America, Europe finally had something China wanted—badly wanted, in fact. Spanish silver became China's money supply. Yet the Chinese court feared that the galleon trade would bring large, uncontrolled changes to Chinese life.

Those fears were correct. Emperor after emperor tried to keep foreigners out of China, but they could not keep out other species. The unexpected arrival of American crops, especially sweet potatoes and corn, led to huge changes in agriculture, migrations within China, deforestation, and floods, as you will see in chapter 6. These changes weakened the Chinese empire—to Europe's benefit.

Across the street from the monument to Legazpi and Urdaneta is another park, where a plaque commemorates Rajah Sulayman, "the brave Muslim ruler" of Manila who refused Legazpi's offer of friendship. When Legazpi approached Sulayman and asked to use Manila's harbor as a launching point for the China trade, Sulayman didn't want the Spaniards around and said no. Legazpi leveled Sulayman's main village, killing him and three hundred others. Modern Manila was established on the ruins. In a sense, Sulayman and his people were the first protesters against globalization. In the end they lost, each and every one, and the process of globalization continues to this day.

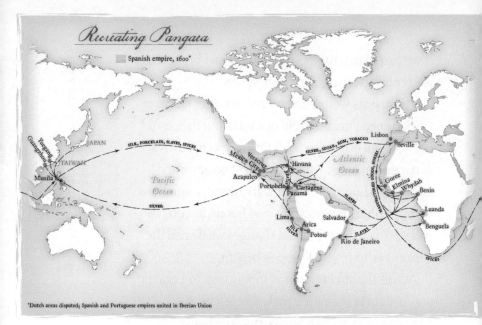

Recreating Pangaea, 1600

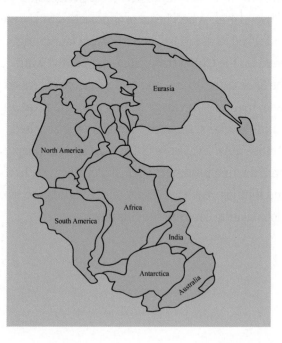

CHAPTER 2

REVERSALS OF FORTUNE

VOYAGES ACROSS THE ATLANTIC AND PACIFIC
suddenly created a world-spanning economic
system. Yet did this really usher in a new era
in the history of life? To answer that question,
imagine flying around the world in 1642, a
century and a half after Columbus's first voyage.
Think of it as a round-the-world cruise at an
altitude of thirty-five thousand feet, above a
planet in the first stages of a great disturbance.
What do the passengers see?

The World in 1642

One thing they see is a world bound together
by hoops of Spanish silver. Silver from Spain's
colonies in the Americas is well on its way to
doubling or tripling the world's stock of precious
metals. From a mountain of silver in Bolivia,
bars and coins travel under guard down the
Andes Mountains to the Pacific Coast to be
loaded onto ships. Military convoys carry the
treasure across the world.

From the plane, follow the silver fleet north,
from its launch point in Peru. To the east are the
Andes Mountains, now in ecological turmoil.
One hundred fifteen years before this flight,
smallpox swept in. Other European diseases
followed, and then the Europeans themselves.
Millions of native people died, and now their
centuries-old farmlands remain empty. Shrubs
and low trees have overwhelmed abandoned
farms. Ecosystems in the Andes, once cultivated,
have gone feral.

Some of the silver vessels anchor in Panama,
while others go on to Mexico. The silver that
goes to Mexico is destined for the China trade.
The silver brought ashore in Panama is carried
across the isthmus of Central America by mule

train to the Atlantic coast, where it is loaded onto ships bound for Europe. Guarded by an armada of galleons bristling with guns and crewed by as many as two thousand seamen and soldiers, the silver crosses the Atlantic every summer, with its departure timed to avoid hurricane season.

Unloaded in Spain, the chests of treasure arrive in a turbulent land. Silver from the Americas has made Europe wealthy and powerful, but from one end to the other the continent is plagued by war, rising prices, rioting, and weather calamities. Turmoil is nothing new in Europe, but this is the first time it is closely linked to the opposite ends of the earth. Trouble flies from Asia, Africa, and the Americas to Europe, shuttling about the world on highways of Spanish silver.

Spain's conquests in the Americas threw its leaders into a fever. Dazed by sudden wealth and power, the Spanish monarchy launched a series of costly wars against other powers in Europe and the Middle East. England was drawn in, and Spain attempted a vast seaborne invasion of England with the Spanish Armada, which failed. War spawned war. In 1642 almost the only European nation not directly at war with Spain is England, which is in the midst of its own civil war.

The costs of all these wars are staggering. To pay for them, the Spanish court borrowed money from foreign bankers, believing that its debts would always be covered by future shipments of American treasure. Debt piled up, and no one wanted to imagine that the good times would end. Yet the result of such a policy is bankruptcy. By 1647, Spain has failed again and again to pay its debts. Worse, the American mines have produced so much silver that its value is falling, even as the production of the mines begins to slow down. The richest nation in the world is hurtling toward financial disaster. Also, because Europe is interconnected in a complex web of economic relationships, Spain's collapse is dragging down its neighbors.

Prices are rising. People are getting poorer— and more desperate. Yet these are not the only problems facing Europe. Instruments aboard the world-circling plane show that the climate itself has been changing.

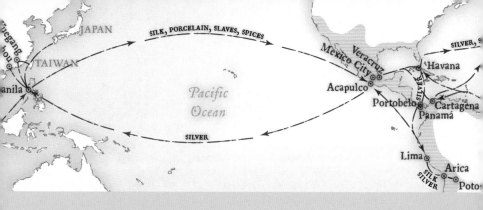

THE CRISIS AND THE POTATO

IN WHAT ECONOMISTS CALL A "PRICE revolution," the cost of living more than doubled across Europe during the last half of the sixteenth century. At least part of the reason was the flood of American silver. The silver bars from Spain's American colonies were turned into silver coins—the "pieces of eight" in old pirate movies. As a result, the amount of money in Spain vastly increased. Prices rose to match, in the process known as inflation.

The cost of living tripled in some places, and then continued to rise in the seventeenth century. Because wages did not keep pace with rising prices, the poor were cast into deep poverty and misery. They could not afford their daily bread. Uprisings of the starving exploded across the continent, seemingly in every corner and all at

once. Researchers have called this the general crisis of the seventeenth century.

Hope for the peasantry came from American crops. By the time of the 1642 round-the-world flight, those crops have ridden the silver route across the Atlantic. They have left the marks of the Columbian Exchange plain to see on the European landscape: plots of American corn in Italy, carpets of American beans in Spain, fields crowded with the shining, upturned faces of American sunflowers in France. Big tobacco leaves soak up sunlight on Dutch farms. Most important will be the potato, which is beginning to fill bellies in Germany, the Netherlands, and, increasingly, Ireland. As you will see in chapter 7, however, dependence on the potato will one day bring its own catastrophic problems.

Climate Change in Reverse

By 1642, the year of our flight, Europe has had almost a century of frighteningly snowy winters, late springs, and cold summers. Rivers freeze. People walk across the frozen sea for a hundred miles from Denmark to Sweden. Harvests are delayed, or fail completely. Food shortages are leading to riots, land seizures, and violence. The order of the world seems overturned.

Historians call this freeze the Little Ice Age. It lasted from about 1550 to 1750 in the Northern Hemisphere, although the time frame is hard to pin down because its effects differed somewhat from one region to the next. Few people at the time kept written records of the weather, so scientists must study the Little Ice Age through indirect measures such as the thickness of tree rings and the chemical makeup of tiny bubbles of gas in polar ice.

Experts have suggested various causes for the Little Ice Age, including sunspots and volcanic eruptions. In 2003 a paleoclimatologist (a specialist in the study of ancient climates) named William F. Ruddiman suggested a different cause. He argued that the Little Ice Age could be explained through a combination of human activity and the Columbian Exchange.

Human communities, Ruddiman pointed out, clear land for farms and cut down trees for fuel and shelter. In Europe and Asia, forests fell to the axe. In the Americas before Columbus, native peoples used fire. Smoke from Indian bonfires shrouded great stretches of North America for weeks on end. The same was true for the grasslands of Argentina, the hills of Mexico, and the high plains of the Andes. Annual fire seasons removed scratchy undergrowth, burned out insect pests, and opened land for farms. Studies at thirty-one archaeological sites in Central and South America found that the amount of charcoal in the soil, a sign of fire, had increased significantly for more than two thousand years.

Then came the Columbian Exchange. Eurasian diseases and parasites swept through the Americas, killing huge numbers of people. This unraveled the land management that Indians had practiced for thousands of years. The flames died out. Open grasslands suddenly filled with forest. In 1634, fourteen years after the Pilgrims landed in Massachusetts, colonist William Wood complained that the once-open forests were now so choked with underbrush as to be "troublesome to travel through." Forests were reborn across large stretches of North America, Central America, the Andes, and the Amazon Basin.

Ruddiman's idea was simple. The destruction of Indian societies by new diseases decreased native burning and increased tree growth. Both these processes took carbon dioxide out of the air. Carbon dioxide is a greenhouse gas, one of the substances that holds heat from the sun inside the earth's atmosphere, warming the planet. If the amount of carbon dioxide drops, less heat is held, and the result is a cooling of the climate. Today scientists warn of climate change, pointing out that the rise in carbon dioxide in the atmosphere is leading to a warmer planet. Ruddiman's idea about the Little Ice Age was today's climate change in reverse, with human action removing greenhouse gases from the atmosphere instead of adding them, creating a cooler planet.

As the plane flies across the Americas, the effects of the Little Ice Age are easy to see. Clearly visible is the filling in of Indian lands by forest—and snow. Boston Harbor and most of Chesapeake Bay are frozen. Horses and cattle, introduced from Europe, die in snowdrifts in Maine and Connecticut. The severe weather nearly wipes out the forty or so French colonists who have just founded Montreal, in Canada.

The plane now swoops south to Mexico and follows the silver fleet to its destination in China. The Little Ice Age has taken hold in East Asia, too. Here it is less a matter of snow and ice than of crashing rain alternating with periods of cold drought, or severe shortage of rain. The five worst years of drought in five centuries occurred between 1637 and 1641, but in this year, 1642, rain is drowning the crops. Everything is made worse by a series of volcanic eruptions in the eastern Pacific. Sulfur dioxide blasted into the atmosphere by volcanoes mixes with water vapor to form tiny droplets of sulfuric acid, which reflects the sun's heat back into space—another thing cooling the climate.

Millions have died. Cold, wet weather and the mass deaths mean that two-thirds of China's farmland is no longer being worked, which adds to the famine. Cannibalism is rumored to be frequent. The court of the Ming dynasty, China's rulers, does little to help. It is paralyzed by infighting and wars to the north. Like the Spanish monarchy, the Ming emperor backs his military ventures with Spanish silver, which his subjects must use to pay their taxes. When the value of silver falls, so does the income from taxes, and the government runs out of money. Mobs of peasant rebels are tearing violently through half a dozen provinces. Within two years the capital, Beijing, will fall to a rebel ex-soldier. This sweeping change in China is just part of larger shift in wealth and power, one that involves the whole world.

From South to North

When Columbus founded La Isabela in 1492, the world's biggest cities clustered in a band around the tropics. All but one of them were within thirty degrees of the equator. At the top of the list was Beijing, followed by Vijayanagar, capital of a Hindu empire in southern India. These were the only cities with as many as half a million people. Below them were Cairo, in Egypt; a handful of cities in China, Iran, and India; Tenochtitlan, the Aztec capital in Mexico; Istanbul, capital of the Islamic Ottoman Empire in what is now Turkey; and possibly Gao, in West Africa, and Qosco, in the Andes. Not a single European city would have made the list of the world's biggest, except maybe Paris. The world was centered on hot places, as it had been ever since the human species, *Homo sapiens*, first stared at the African sky.

A century and a half later, in 1642, that order

PART ONE: ONE WORLD

is changing. It is as if the globe has been turned upside down and all the wealth and power are flowing from south to north. The once-great metropolises of the tropics are falling into ruin. In the coming centuries, the great cities will all be in the milder climate zone of the north: London and Manchester in Britain; New York, Chicago, and Philadelphia in the United States. By 1900 all the world's most populous cities will be in Europe or the United States except one, Tokyo, the most Westernized of Eastern cities.

To an observer from space, the change would have seemed shocking. The order of human affairs for thousands of years had been overturned— at least for a while. To us today, the tumult of ecological and economic exchange is like the background radiation of our ever more crowded and unstable planet. We have grown used to it. We are not surprised to find Japanese loggers in Brazil, Chinese engineers in West Africa, or Europeans backpacking in Nepal or dining in New York. Yet, in different ways, these kinds of exchanges also happened hundreds of years ago. They are how we got to where we are today.

(right)
Tenochtitlan dazzled the Spaniards when they saw it. The city was grander than any in Spain. A ten-mile-long dike (far right in image) separated the salty water of the main lake from a new, human-made freshwater lake that provided water for artificial wetland farms known as *chinampas.*

PART TWO

ATLANTIC
JOURNEYS

THE COLUMBIAN EXCHANGE THAT RESHAPED the world began with voyages across the Atlantic Ocean. Money and biology were closely intertwined in the exchange from the start. Jamestown, the beginning of permanent English colonization in the Americas, was founded as a purely economic venture. Its fate, however, was decided by ecological forces, especially the introduction of tobacco, which originated along the lower reaches of the Amazon River. This habit-forming plant became the subject of the first truly worldwide craze for a product. Yet it was the microscopic creatures that cause malaria and yellow fever, more than any other introduced species, that shaped American societies from Baltimore to Buenos Aires. These tiny newcomers had huge effects on matters ranging from slavery in Virginia to poverty in South America. Part Two closes with a look at the role malaria played in the creation of the United States.

CHAPTER 3

THE TOBACCO COAST

EARTHWORMS DID NOT EXIST IN MUCH OF
North America before 1492. In New England
and the upper Midwest, for example, the last ice
age had wiped them out. After the ice melted,
worms from the south had not moved north
because earthworms do not travel long distances
unless carried by humans. When Europeans
unknowingly introduced two species of
earthworms, the common night crawler and the
red marsh worm, they dramatically changed the
North American forest ecosystem.

In worm-free woodlands, leaves pile up
on the forest floor. When earthworms are
introduced, they chew through this leaf litter
in months, packing its nutrients away into
the soil in the form of their waste. Trees and
shrubs that depend on leaf litter begin to die off,

and the forest becomes drier and more open. Earthworms compete for food with small insects and drive down their numbers. The birds, lizards, and mammals that feed off these small insects in the leaf litter decline, too.

Where did the night crawler and marsh worm first squirm onto American soil? Possibly in the Jamestown colony in Virginia, kicking off what one worm researcher has called a "gigantic, unplanned ecological experiment" four hundred years in the making.

Romantic tales surround Jamestown. The most famous story tells how the Indian maiden Pocahontas saved the life of John Smith, one of the leaders of the Jamestown colony. Most researchers today believe that story to be untrue. Less well known is the fact that although Smith and other brave adventurers were vital to the success of Jamestown, the colony was founded as a business venture, not a base for exploration or heroic deeds.

Like La Isabela in the Caribbean, Jamestown was supposed to be a trading post. The first permanent English colony in North America was an attempt by merchants to snatch up the vast stores of silver and gold they imagined

(left)
A ten-year-old boy "worming" tobacco on a farm in Kentucky, 1916. The worms— actually, the larvae of moths—were peeled off the leaves one-by-one to protect the crop.

existed around Jamestown, in the big, shallow Chesapeake Bay. Equally important, the merchants wanted to find a route through North America, which they imagined was only a few hundred miles wide, less than a month's journey. When they came to the Pacific coast, they would be able to sail to China, which was the colony's ultimate reason for existence. Jamestown's founders intended to bring isolated Virginia into the world market—to globalize it and give England a share of the China trade.

The merchants behind the Virginia colony were wrong about the silver and gold. They were also wrong about the easy route to China. They did not realize that three thousand miles of forests, prairies, deserts, and mountains lay between Jamestown and the Pacific. Purely as a business venture, Jamestown was a disaster. Yet the colony left a big mark. It launched the great struggles over democracy and slavery that would be important in the future United States.

The Jamestown colony was also the beginning of the Columbian Exchange in English America. In biological terms, the colony marks the point when *before* turns into *after*. Setting up camp on the marshy Jamestown peninsula, the colonists were bringing the new age of global interconnectedness to North America without realizing it. Jamestown was a brushfire in a planetary ecological firestorm. The earthworms were just the beginning.

A Risky Venture

La Isabela, Columbus's doomed first attempt to establish a trading post in the Caribbean, had been funded and controlled by the Spanish monarchy. Jamestown was different. It was a private business, sponsored by a group of people with money and political connections who formed the Virginia Company, pooling their resources to pay for a commercial venture in return for shares of the profits. Jamestown was founded in this way because England's rulers, Queen Elizabeth I and King James I, who followed Elizabeth on the throne, wanted the benefits of trade and conquest but couldn't pay for them. Nor could the monarchy borrow the necessary cash, because moneylenders' interest rates were ruinously high. True, kings and queens had the power to force loans from their subjects, but that practice was deeply unpopular.

It would be sure to create discontent among the people. Was the gamble of an American colony worth it?

Elizabeth and James came to the same conclusion: no.

Colonization was risky. The English faced the additional danger that most of the Americas had already been claimed by Spain. Hostility between the two nations was intense. After Elizabeth died in 1603, James lowered the tension, but he knew that an English colony in North America would rekindle the conflict. Spain had already planted a string of small colonies and missions on the Atlantic Coast. One was just miles away from Jamestown's future location. (It failed.) If that weren't enough, France had also claimed North America.

Still, the English monarchs were unwilling to give up the Americas to the competition. They had seen how richly Spain was rewarded with the silver of Mexico and South America. Also there was opportunity in North America, or so people thought. Many powerful Londoners believed that a watery channel cut across North America, and that it would be possible to sail through what is now the United

States to reach the Pacific Ocean—and China on its other side. Elizabeth and James therefore turned the task and risk of establishing a North American colony over to the Virginia Company, whose three small ships set sail from London to Virginia in 1606.

Strange Land

On May 14, 1607, the ships anchored in the James River. In movies and textbooks, the Jamestown colonists are often shown arriving in a pristine forest of ancient trees, with small bands of Indians gliding like silent ghosts beneath the canopy. This image sees the colonists as "settlers" in an empty land. In fact, the English ships landed in the middle of a small but rapidly growing Indian empire called Tsenacomoco.

Thirty years before, Tsenacomoco had been six small, separate clusters of villages. By the time the foreigners came from overseas, its ruler, Powhatan, had tripled its area. Dozens of villages scattered through the forest east of Chesapeake Bay housed more than fourteen thousand people. One historical geographer believes that Tsenacomoco may have had a larger

population in 1600 than equal-size areas of western Europe.

Powhatan's people—the "Powhatan Indians," as the newcomers called them—lived in settlements of a few hundred people, surrounded by fields where corn, beans, squash, and melons were all grown together. No fences protected these mixed fields, because the Powhatan had no livestock to protect their crops from. (The Americas, by a quirk of biological history, had few animals that could be domesticated.) Instead, the Indians scattered their farm plots within larger cleared areas where they gathered useful wild plants, such as grains, edible greens, and medicinal herbs. The English did not understand that these areas for gathering were useful. From their point of view, the Powhatan landscape was a bewildering jumble of "unused" land and unfenced, messy farms. To the English, well-kept fences and neat plantings of single crops were a sign of civilization. It seemed to them that the Indians did not truly occupy the land because they had not "improved" it in the English style.

The land around the Chesapeake was a patchwork of bogs, marshes, grassy ponds, slow-

(left)
The only known likeness of Powhatan created in his lifetime is this sketch ornamenting a 1612 map by John Smith. In his longhouse Powhatan smokes a tobacco pipe, surrounded by his wives and advisors.

moving streams, and meadows that flooded in certain seasons. This soggy landscape, which was unfamiliar to the English, had been shaped by the dam-building American beaver, whose constructions turn streams into ponds and wetlands, smearing water across the landscape. Surrounding the cleared areas and the marshes was the forest. Unlike English forest reserves, which were kept mostly wild, the Chesapeake forests had been shaped by Indian fires. Every fall, the underbrush was burned so that tender new growth would attract deer, elk, and moose for the Indians to hunt. Because this burning killed brush and young trees, the forest that the English colonists encountered was a soaring woodland of huge, widely spaced trees—a beautiful sight, but just as artificial as the burned-off clearings where corn was planted.

Like the English countryside that the colonists had left behind, Chesapeake Bay had been made by its inhabitants into a working landscape. Just as the tidy checkerboard of fenced fields was essential to English culture, the crazy-quilt patchwork of ecological zones in coastal Virginia was essential to the Powhatan way of life. Yet the English newcomers saw only a random

(left)
Rather than covering fenced plots with neat rows of wheat, the Powhatan planted many crops at once, as in this replica of a Wendat (Huron) garden. The English newcomers often couldn't recognize native farms and gardens as cultivated land.

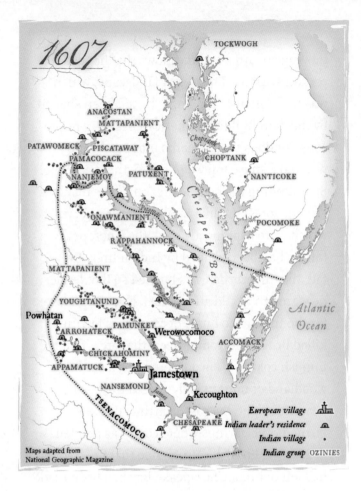

1607

TOCKWOGH

ANACOSTAN
MATTAPANIENT

PATAWOMECK   PISCATAWAY
PAMACOCACK   *Choptank*
NANJEMOY   PATUXENT   CHOPTANK
                                      NANTICOKE

ONAWMANIENT   POCOMOKE

RAPPAHANNOCK

MATTAPANIENT   *Chesapeake Bay*

YOUGHTANUND   *Atlantic Ocean*

Powhatan
ARROHATECK
PAMUNKEY   Werowocomoco
CHICKAHOMINY   ACCOMACK
APPAMATUCK
              Jamestown
NANSEMOND
              Kecoughton

TSENACOMOCO   CHESAPEAKE

European village
Indian leader's residence
Indian village
Indian group OZINIES

Maps adapted from
National Geographic Magazine

Even the groundwa-
ter was salty. The
U.S. government
suggests that salt
levels should not ex-
ceed 20 milligrams
per liter; Jamestown
had more than twen-
ty times that much.
Other settlements
had even more.

66

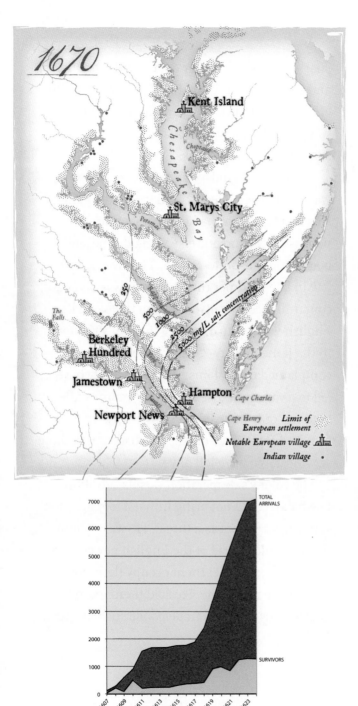

1670

Kent Island

Chesapeake

Choptank

St. Marys City

Patuxent

250

500

1000

2500

5000 mg/L salt concentration

The Falls

Berkeley Hundred

Jamestown

Hampton   Cape Charles

Newport News   Cape Henry   Limit of European settlement

Notable European village 🏛

Indian village •

Jamestown was founded within the small empire of Tsenacomoco. Rivers served as the empire's highways. Because the water at the river mouths was salty, Tsenacomoco villages were mostly upstream. The English put Jamestown as far upriver as they could—but not far enough to avoid the bad water.

TOTAL ARRIVALS

7000

6000

5000

4000

3000

2000

1000

0

SURVIVORS

1607 1609 1611 1613 1615 1617 1619 1621 1623

Most of the thousands of hopeful English who came to Virginia quickly died. This chart shows the author's best attempt to calculate the total number of migrants and Jamestown's actual population every year. The overall picture is clear—and dismaying.

67

snarl of marshes, beaver ponds, unkempt fields, and hostile forest. If the English wanted to live and prosper in this new land in the way they were used to, they would have to change it into something more suitable.

All the good land along the James River was already occupied by Indian villages. The Virginia Company had to plant its colony on a peninsula that no one else wanted. The site was boggy and mosquito-ridden. The river fell so low in late summer that the water was stagnant, contaminated by saltwater from the bay. The English wound up drinking the foulest water in the James River—"full of slime and filth," complained one colonist. Bad water may have led to a variety of diseases. Eight months after landing, only thirty-eight of the more than one hundred English colonists who had come ashore at Jamestown were left alive.

The colony's desperation was its salvation. Powhatan could not bring himself to regard the starving strangers as a threat. He was certain that he could get rid of the English newcomers at any time, so he let them occupy their not-so-valuable real estate. He sold them grain as long as they provided trade goods such as guns, axes, knives, mirrors, glass beads, and sheets of copper.

New shiploads of colonists arrived, but soon violence broke out between the English and the Indians, and Powhatan stopped providing the colony with food. The English had stockpiled no supplies and were reduced to eating "dogs, cats, rats and mice"—and the corpses of the dead. By the spring of 1610 only about sixty colonists had survived what was called the "starving time."

Just as the survivors were about to abandon the colony, more shiploads of colonists and supplies arrived. Year after year, the Virginia Company spent large sums to send colonists to Virginia—more than a hundred shiploads in total. Year after year, most would-be settlers died within weeks or months. Even after the first hope of finding precious metals and a route to Asia did not pan out, why did the company keep sending ship after doomed ship? Equally puzzling, why did Powhatan let the colony survive?

Part of the answer to both questions is the Columbian Exchange.

Boom and Bust

Pocahontas, a daughter of Powhatan who had been kidnapped by the Jamestown colonists, married one of them, John Rolfe, in 1614. The wedding brought a cease-fire to the hostilities between the English and the Powhatan. Around that time, Powhatan's brother Opechancanough took over as ruler of the tribe. Under his guidance, Indians studied the ways of the English. They traded with the English, served in their militias, stockpiled their guns—and secretly prepared to attack them.

The colonists were unaware of Opechancanough's scheme, but they were unleashing a devastating counterattack against the Indians without even realizing it. That counterattack was the Columbian Exchange. One of its most powerful weapons was tobacco.

Tobacco had been unknown in Europe until Spaniards brought the plant back from the Caribbean. Exotic and addictive, it had swiftly become a craze among the aristocrats of Europe. By 1616, according to one estimate, London alone had more than seven thousand tobacco "houses," café-like places where the city's growing throng of nicotine junkies could buy and smoke tobacco.

(right)
This 1616 engraving of Pocahontas was made during her visit to England. It is the only known full portrait of a Powhatan.

MATOAKA ALS REBECCA FILIA POTENTISS PRINC POWHATANI IMP VIRGINIÆ.

Ætatis suæ 21. A.
1616.

(The profoundly destructive effects of tobacco on human health, especially on the lungs, would not be proven until centuries later. However, some authorities did try to ban it early on because they believed it to be unhealthful, or immoral, or disturbing to the social order.)

Unfortunately for the English, at first the only source of fine tobacco was the American colonies of hated Spain. London tobacco houses were thrilled by the sudden appearance of tobacco leaves from the Jamestown colony. Tobacco was shipped across the Atlantic in huge barrels that held half a ton or more. Those barrels were carried back to Virginia full of ballast—that is, packed with dirt to give them weight and keep the ships stable. Dumped on Virginian shores, that ballast very possibly contained the earthworms that made themselves at home in North America.

The native tobacco of Virginia was the species *Nicotiana rustica*. It was much less desirable to the English and Europeans than the species found in South America and the Caribbean, which is *Nicotiana tabacum*. John Rolfe talked a shipmaster into bringing him some *N. tabacum* seeds, and soon that variety of tobacco was

growing in the Virginia colony. After Rolfe's
marriage to Pocahontas created the cease-fire
with the Indians, the colonists were able to
expand tobacco production explosively.

By 1620, Jamestown was shipping fifty
thousand pounds of tobacco a year. Three years
later the figure had almost tripled. Within
forty years the Chesapeake Bay—the Tobacco
Coast, as it later became known—was exporting
twenty-five million pounds of tobacco a year.
Individual farmers were making profits of
up to 1,000 percent on their investments.
Newcomers poured in, grabbed some land, and
planted *N. tabacum*. English-style farms spread
like rumors up and down the James and York
Rivers. So many colonists flooded Virginia that
the company realized it could not control them
completely from across the ocean. In 1619 it
created an elected council to resolve disputes.
This was the first representative governing body
in colonial North America.

Barely three weeks later, a Dutch pirate ship
landed at Jamestown. It carried some twenty
African slaves. (Another thirty showed up in a
second ship a few days later.) The colonists had
been clamoring for more workers to increase

their tobacco crop and profits. Without a second thought, they bought the Africans in exchange for food the pirates needed. The purchase was a landmark on the road to slavery.

Within weeks, Jamestown had begun two of the longest-lasting institutions of the future United States. One was representative democracy, in which people have a say in their government. The other was chattel slavery, in which human beings are bought and sold as property.

The tobacco boom came too late for the Virginia Company. It had exhausted its resources and run up debts sending ship after ship across the ocean in the first years of the colony. The company was running out of money on March 22, 1622, when Opechancanough attacked Jamestown.

The assault was brutal, widespread, and well planned. At least 325 people were killed that day, and the aftermath claimed at least 700 more. The attack disrupted spring planting, so the colonists planted less corn than usual. Trying to rebuild, the company sent over more than 1,000 new colonists—but no food supplies. The luckless souls were dumped ashore, where they

(top right)
This image is inaccurate in many ways—the neatly walled fortress in the distance is unlike Jamestown or any Powhatan settlement—but it still captures a sense of the shock caused by the Powhatan attack on Virginia in 1622.

(bottom right)
After the Virginia Indians were defeated in the 1660s, they were required to wear identifying badges to enter English settlements. This badge belonged to a native leader.

were forced to eat tree bark and scrabble over handfuls of corn. It was the "starving time" all over again. About two out of three Europeans in Virginia died that year.

The Virginia Company did not survive this disaster. Yet English settlement in Virginia did. Although Opechancanough's assault was a setback, the English had begun reshaping the landscape into something unrecognizable to the Indians.

Indians had traditionally raised small amounts of tobacco in their gardens. The English, in contrast, covered big areas with tobacco farms. Planting tobacco on a massive scale has a massive environmental impact. Tobacco absorbs the nutrients nitrogen and potassium, removing them from the soil. As they harvested and exported tobacco, the English were sending those nutrients away on ships. Soils in Chesapeake Bay were thin and easily exhausted. By planting huge areas with tobacco, the English quickly wore out their fields. As a result, they felt the constant push to clear new land.

The colonists quickly grabbed most of the land that had been cleared by the Indians, then moved into the forest, cutting great numbers of trees. Removing trees and using plows exposed the soil and made it vulnerable. Rain washed away nutrients. When dry, land without tree cover eroded more quickly. With fewer trees to capture and hold rain, floods were suddenly more common. It became harder and harder for the Indians to find suitable areas to farm, so they moved farther into the interior, giving up the coast to the foreigners.

Tobacco from South America was far from the only biological import to Virginia. Pigs, goats, cattle, and horses multiplied. The colonists lost control of their animals, which devoured Indian gardens. The worst may have been the pigs. Smart, strong, and always hungry, rampaging pigs ate the fruits, nuts, corn, and edible bulbs that made up the Indian diet. The people of Tsenacomoco found themselves competing for their food supply with packs of feral pigs.

In the long run, though, the biggest impact may have come from a much smaller imported creature: the European honeybee. The English imported bees for honey. They did not know that bees also pollinated crops. The bees pollinated anyway. Without their invisible work, many of the plants that Europeans brought to North America, including peaches, apples, and watermelons, wouldn't have multiplied.

Removing trees, introducing bees and earthworms, exhausting the soil, shutting down the annual burning, unleashing pigs and other grazing and rooting animals—in these ways the colonists changed Tsenacomoco so much that it became harder and harder for the Indians to prosper there, but easier and easier for the Europeans. By 1650 the former Tsenacomoco Empire was mainly inhabited by Europeans.

Sea of China and the Indies.

Sir Francis Drake *was on this sea and landed* An° 1577 in 37 deg: where hee tooke Possession in the name of Q: Eliza: Calling it new Albion.

Whose happy shores, (in ten dayes march with 50 foote and 30 horsmen from the head of Iames River, over those hills and through the rich adjacent Vallyes beautyfied with as profitable rivers, which necessarily must run into ye peacefull Indian sea) may be discovered. to the exceeding benefit of Great Brittain, and joye of all true English.

Scala Miliarum

A mapp of Virginia discouered to ye in ti' Latt: From 35 deg: &.½ Florida, to 41 deg: bounds of new

Mangoack C.

Mankes C.

The falls

Carolana

VIRGINIA, & new

"THE GREATEST ERROR"

JOHN FERRAR WAS A WEALTHY LONDONER who invested in the Virginia Company and later found himself in charge of its finances. The company was making money from tobacco sales but had piled up so much debt that Ferrar had to scramble to pay its bills. Worse, he claimed, the previous management had stolen a large sum of company funds. When Ferrar tried to recover the money, the thieves attempted to smear him in court. The Indian attack on Jamestown in 1622 gave the company's enemies a chance to make accusations against Ferrar and his brother, the company's secretary. The two were portrayed as reckless swindlers and thrown in jail. They managed to talk their way free, but the king put an end to the Virginia Company.

Maps like this one were common in seventeenth-century Europe. North America was thought to be a narrow strip of land. The Virginia Company's English backers believed their colonists at Jamestown could easily walk to the Pacific then sail to China.

The failure of the company ate at John Ferrar long afterward. Twenty-five years later, when he read a book about the Virginia colony that blamed him and other managers for Jamestown's troubles, he filled the margins with angry notes. To Ferrar, the colony's biggest mistake had not been failing to plant wheat in addition to tobacco, as some critics said. The real mistake had been ignoring the goal of cutting through the North American continent and pioneering a new route to the Pacific.

Failure to find that sea highway to Asia, Ferrar wrote, "is to this day the greatest Error and damadge that hath happened to the Collony all this while." He was certain that a march of only eight or ten days, maybe just four days, separated Jamestown from the Pacific Ocean.

A single expedition west would have discovered "Soe Infinite a Riches to them all as a passadge to a West Sea would prove to them." Instead, the Jamestown colonists had stupidly filled their days with "Smokey Tobacco."

Yet the goal of the Virginia Company had been to bring Virginia, and cash-strapped England, into the global marketplace. Although Ferrar never recognized it, the company had done exactly that—with "Smokey Tobacco," the first American species to spread into Europe, Asia, and Africa.

Tobacco's Long Reach

Exciting and wildly addictive, tobacco was an instant hit around the globe. For the first time, people in every continent fell under the spell of a new product at the same time. Tobacco was the leading edge of the Columbian Exchange.

By the time Jamestown was founded in 1607, tobacco had already circled the globe, carried in Spanish ships. A traveler in Sierra Leone, in West Africa, saw that tobacco, likely brought by slave traders, could be found in every house. In Japan, group smoke-ins by violent young men in the city of Edo (later known as Tokyo) led to the formation of two rival gangs, called the Bramble Club and the Leather-breeches Club. After throwing seventy of the club members in jail, the shogun, or imperial military commander, banned smoking. In Manchuria, on the northern border of China, nicotine addiction quickly became so widespread that in 1635 the khan, or king, discovered that his soldiers were selling their weapons to buy tobacco. Like the shogun, the khan angrily banned smoking. In Delhi, India, tobacco enthralled the upper classes. The first smoker in Delhi, to the dismay of his advisers, was the emperor.

On the opposite side of the world, Europeans were equally hooked. By the 1640s the Vatican, center of the Roman Catholic Church, was getting complaints that priests were celebrating Mass with lighted cigars. Pope Urban VIII, as enraged as the khan of Manchuria, promptly banned smoking in church.

From Beijing to Boston to Bristol, people became part of an international culture of tobacco. Virginia played a small but important part in creating this worldwide phenomenon. From today's point of view, though, tobacco was less important in itself than as a magnet that pulled many other nonhuman creatures across the Atlantic Ocean in the ongoing Columbian Exchange. Two of the most important of these creatures were tiny travelers that played a devastating role in American life.

CHAPTER 4

EVIL AIR

IN HIS ACCOUNT OF HIS SECOND VOYAGE TO the Caribbean, Christopher Columbus wrote that "all my people went ashore to settle, and everyone realized that it rained a lot. They became gravely ill from *çiçiones*." The term *çiçiones* refers to a bout of illness that begins with chills, followed by days of high fever and weakness. One of the many diseases that cause chills and fevers is malaria, which is spread through mosquito bites.

Did Columbus's men get malaria? If so, they brought it with them. Malaria in humans did not exist in the Americas before Europeans arrived. Historians do not know for certain that the disease that attacked Columbus's people in 1493 was malaria, but if just one of his men had malaria and suffered an attack after landing in Hispaniola, it would have taken only one

(left)
A mosquito-net headdress fashioned in the early twentieth century.

85

bite by the right type of mosquito to spread the disease from that victim to others—and those mosquitoes are abundant on Hispaniola.

Malaria is responsible for unimaginable suffering. In spite of a worldwide effort to wipe out malaria that began in the 1950s, the disease still infects some twenty million people each year and kills more than six hundred thousand. Most of those who die are children under the age of five. Those who don't die can be sickened and weakened for months, even with modern medical care. The disease can lurk in the body for months and then emerge with another full-scale attack. So many people in Africa suffer so often from malaria that economists think the disease has seriously slowed the pace of development there.

As it does today, malaria played a huge role in the past. Its role was different from that of other diseases, and maybe larger. When Europeans brought smallpox and influenza to the Americas, they set off epidemics, sudden outbursts that shot through Indian towns and villages and then faded. Malaria became endemic, which means that it was always present in the landscape. Instead of coming in sudden, severe bursts, malaria was a constant, steady background to life.

Malaria and yellow fever (another disease brought to the Americas, also carried by mosquitoes) turned the Americas upside down. Before these diseases arrived, the most thickly populated area north of Mexico was what is now the southeastern United States—Georgia, the Carolinas, Alabama. To the south, the wet forests of southern Mexico, Central America, and the Amazon Basin held millions of people. After malaria and yellow fever, these previously healthful areas became inhospitable as the diseases thrived. The Indians who had lived there fled to safer ground.

Europeans who moved into the emptied real estate often died within a year. These deaths had a long-lasting effect. Even today, the places where European colonists couldn't survive are poorer than places they found more healthful. That's because Europeans created different institutions in disease areas than in healthful areas. In healthful areas, they built stable colonies that attracted settlers. The growing populations of these areas included farmers, craftspeople, and business owners. Schools, roads, hospitals, legal codes, and government systems were put in place. Disease areas, however, attracted smaller numbers of Europeans. There the colonizers had little interest in building functioning social and government institutions. Instead they focused on using native or captive labor to remove resources such as timber, precious metals, or crops that were grown on plantations and exported.

Disease played a part in how the labor force in the American colonies developed. Because malaria and yellow fever killed European and Indian workers in the tobacco and sugar plantations of the Americas, the colonists imported labor in the form of captive Africans— the human side of the Columbian Exchange. The ecological exchange, in the form of new diseases, led to the economic exchange, in the form of slavery. In turn, slavery had political effects that have continued to the present day.

It would be an exaggeration to say that malaria and yellow fever were responsible for the slave trade, or that they are the reason the weak, divided thirteen colonies won independence from mighty Great Britain in the Revolutionary War. Yet as you will see in this chapter, it would not be completely wrong, either.

(right)
Single-celled *Plasmodium* parasites burst out of dying red blood cells, beginning the assault on the body that leads to full-blown malaria.

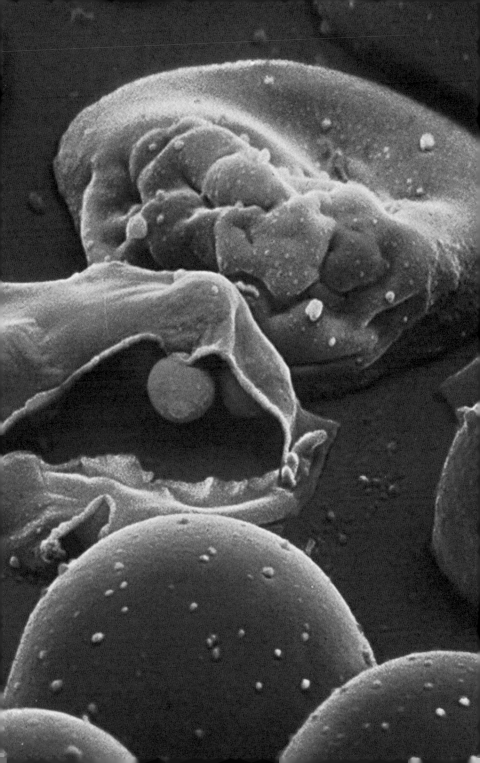

The Mystery of Malaria

In Columbus's day, people did not realize that malaria was a specific disease. They thought of it as a collection of symptoms, and they believed it was caused by marshy or bad air. The English word malaria, in fact, comes from the Italian *mal aria*, meaning "evil or bad air."

Malaria, however, is a disease with a complicated life cycle that was not understood until modern times. It is caused by two hundred or so species of microscopic parasites that plague countless types of reptiles, birds, and mammals. Four of those parasite species target human beings—and they are dishearteningly good at their jobs.

Each parasite consists of a single cell. It is injected into human flesh by the bite of a mosquito. Once in the body, the parasite pries open red blood cells and climbs inside. Floating around the circulatory system like passengers in submarines, the parasites reproduce in huge numbers inside the infected red blood cells. Eventually they burst out and pour into the bloodstream. Most of the parasites force their way into new red blood cells, but a few drift in the blood, waiting to be sucked up by a mosquito. When a mosquito takes in the parasite, the parasite reproduces again inside the insect. Parasites squirm into the mosquito's saliva glands, where they wait to be injected into a new host when the mosquito bites someone.

Inside the human body, most of the infected red blood cells release their parasites at about the same time. Infection from a single malaria parasite can produce *ten billion* new ones. These huge assaults overwhelm the host's immune system, setting off spasms of chills and fever. Eventually the host's immune system beats back the attack, but within days a new attack takes place because some of the previous wave of parasites have hidden themselves inside red blood cells and produced a new generation of billions of parasites. This cycle repeats until the immune system finally defeats the parasite. It may not be a real victory, though. The parasites can hide in other corners of the body, only to emerge again weeks later. The sign of full-blown malaria is half a dozen episodes of chills and fever, followed by a short period of relief, and then another wave of attacks.

The two most widespread forms of malaria in humans are caused by the microorganisms

Plasmodium vivax and *Plasmodium falciparum*. Their symptoms are similar, but they have different effects on the body. *P. falciparum* can cut off circulation to the kidneys, lungs, brain, and other organs. Organ failure kills as many as one out of ten *P. falciparum* sufferers. *P. vivax* doesn't destroy organs, which makes it less deadly, but during its attacks sufferers are weak, and vulnerable to other diseases. With both types of malaria, sufferers can be sick for months at a time, and they are infectious during attacks. A mosquito that bites a sick malaria sufferer can transfer the disease to others.

Plasmodium microorganisms are tropical and sensitive to temperature. The speed at which they can reproduce inside mosquitoes depends on the temperature of the outside air. As the days get colder, it takes the parasite longer and longer to reproduce, until it takes longer than the mosquito's lifespan—which ends the cycle. Practically speaking, *P. falciparum* cannot survive and reproduce for long below temperatures of about 66 degrees Fahrenheit. *P. vivax* has a limit of about 59 degrees.

P. falciparum thrives in most of Africa. In Europe it gained a foothold only in the warmest areas: Greece, Italy, Portugal, and southern Spain. *P. vivax*, however, became endemic in most of Europe, including cooler northern places such as England, the Netherlands, and southern Scandinavia. *P. falciparum* came to the Americas from Africa and was spread by Africans. *P. vivax* came from Europe and was spread by Europeans. This difference had historic consequences.

The Mosquito Connection

Human malaria is carried only by mosquitoes in the *Anopheles* genus. (A genus is a group of closely related species.) Landscape engineering by humans in sixteenth-century England created the perfect conditions for *Anopheles* mosquitoes and vivax malaria to prosper—and be carried to the Americas by English colonists.

The mosquitoes that carry malaria, and the disease itself, seem to have been rare in England until the later sixteenth century. At that time, Queen Elizabeth I began encouraging landlords to drain marshes and other wetlands to create more farmland. A great deal of drainage work was done in the coastal wetlands of eastern and southeastern England. Much of this low,

ANOPHELES MACULIPENNIS. ♂

(MEIGEN)

E.Wilson, Cambridge

foggy landscape had been flooded regularly by the high tides of the North Sea, which washed away mosquito larvae before they could hatch into adult mosquitoes. The work of draining the wetlands blocked the sea but left the land dotted with pockets of standing water that were not scoured by the tides. These pools were the perfect habitat for *Anopheles* mosquitoes.

Farmers moved into the former marshlands, which were still soggy but now usable for farming. They heated their homes and barns during cold weather, providing a place for the mosquito, and the *P. vivax* parasites inside it, to survive the cold weather, ready to breed and spread the following spring. Church records show that in the 1570s, before the draining of the marshes, baptisms outnumbered burials in twenty-four wetland parishes. In other words, the population was rising. Two decades later, with draining in full swing, the trend had reversed. There were almost twice as many burials as baptisms. Population was booming in other parts of England, but these wetland parishes would not return to their earlier rates of growth for almost two centuries. Clergymen died in such numbers after being sent to

(left)
Mosquitos in the *Anopheles* genus carry human malaria.

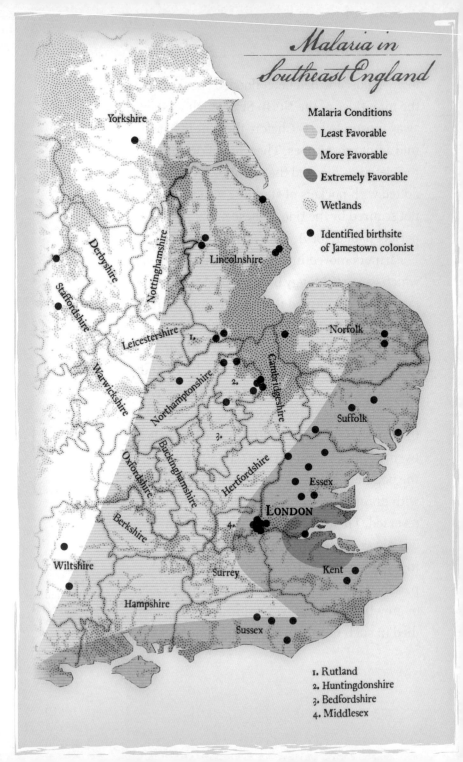

Malaria in Southeast England

Malaria Conditions

- Least Favorable
- More Favorable
- Extremely Favorable
- Wetlands
- Identified birthsite of Jamestown colonist

Yorkshire

Derbyshire

Staffordshire

Nottinghamshire

Lincolnshire

Leicestershire

Warwickshire

Norfolk

1.

Northamptonshire

2.

Cambridgeshire

Suffolk

Oxfordshire

Buckinghamshire

3.

Hertfordshire

Essex

Berkshire

4.

LONDON

Wiltshire

Surrey

Kent

Hampshire

Sussex

1. Rutland
2. Huntingdonshire
3. Bedfordshire
4. Middlesex

southeast England that the region became known as Killpriest.

Draining the marshes of eastern and southeastern England set off an inferno of vivax malaria. The English wetlands were not the only area affected, however. There is good reason to think that vivax malaria traveled from there to the North American colonies. Information about the early colonists is sketchy and incomplete, but one researcher has estimated that about 60 percent of the first wave of English immigrants to North America came from nine counties in eastern and southeastern England—the country's malaria belt.

One example is the hundred-plus colonists who began Jamestown. Fifty-nine of their birthplaces are known. Thirty-seven of those fifty-nine came from malaria-ridden counties. Even if most of them set off from higher, inland parts of the counties that had less malaria than the coastal wetlands, some of them would have come from the marshes. Those who didn't come from the malaria zone usually passed through it just before departure, as their ships waited for weeks or even months at points along the Thames River that were malaria centers.

People in the midst of malarial attacks would seem to be unlikely candidates for a difficult sea voyage. Yet *Plasmodium* can hide inside a seemingly healthy person. Colonists could board their ships without symptoms, land in Chesapeake Bay country, and then be struck by the teeth-chattering chills and sweat-bursting fevers of malaria. At that point, unfortunately, they could pass the parasite to every mosquito that bit them—and waiting on the East Coast of North America were five *Anopheles* species that became the primary spreaders of the disease.

Malaria in the Americas

"In theory, one person could have established the parasite in the entire continent [of North America]," said Andrew Spielman, a malaria researcher at the Harvard School of Public Health. "It's a bit like throwing darts. Bring enough sick people in contact with enough mosquitoes and sooner or later you'll hit the bull's-eye—you'll establish malaria."

Almost certainly some of the colonists at Jamestown, Virginia, were infectious. If the disease started there, it soon spread north.

By 1657, John Winthrop, the governor of the Connecticut colony, was recording cases of malaria symptoms. Researchers now think that malaria entered the continent in the 1640s or even earlier. Conditions for the disease were perfect between 1606 and 1612, when low-lying coastal Virginia suffered a series of droughts. These droughts would have turned flowing streams into strings of little standing pools, the ideal habitat for mosquito larvae. The Jamestown settlement was founded in 1607, in the heart of the drought period.

Whenever malaria arrived, it rapidly made itself at home in Virginia. It became as unavoidable there as it was in the English marshes. Everyone expected new arrivals to get sick and to be fairly useless for the first year, until they were "seasoned"—in other words, until they had battled malaria and won. The battle often ended in the cemetery, however. During Jamestown's first half century, as many as a third of new arrivals died within a year. After that, Virginians learned by trial and error to live with vivax. They avoided marshes and stayed indoors at dusk, when mosquitoes are most active. Malaria-related deaths among new arrivals fell from 20 or 30 percent around 1650 to 10 percent or lower around 1670. These numbers reflect a considerable improvement, but still much suffering.

The story of New Edinburgh shows the big role that disease played in colonization. You've probably never heard of New Edinburgh, even though it was a large, ambitious colonial venture. That's because it was also a short-lived disaster.

New Edinburgh was meant to be a Scottish colony in Panama. The colony's organizer claimed that the location, on the narrow strip of land that separates the Atlantic and Pacific Oceans, would let the colony control "at least two-thirds" of the Asia trade with Europe. Dazzled by this vision, more than fourteen hundred people in Scotland put money into a joint-stock venture, the same type of business organization that had founded Jamestown. Scotland was a poor nation. Historians estimate that the investments in New Edinburgh amounted to between a quarter and half of all the available money in the country.

In 1698 five ships set sail with twelve hundred colonists and a year's food supply. They landed on the coast of Panama and started clearing forest to build the port of New Edinburgh. Just eight months later the ragged survivors (fewer than three hundred people) bolted for home. They reached Scotland just days after a second expedition of four ships and thirteen hundred people had left for Panama. Nine months later that second expedition also fled. Not a hundred people made it home. Lost with the dead was every penny invested in the venture.

Why did New Edinburgh fail? There were many reasons. Planning to trade with the local Indians, the colonists had stuffed their ships with Scotland's finest products: woolen hose and blankets, ornamental wigs, and twenty-five thousand pairs of leather shoes. Alas, it proved difficult to sell warm socks and itchy blankets in the tropics. Meanwhile, hard tropical rains washed away the colonists' supplies and their efforts to farm. To make matters worse, Spain, which had already established colonies in Central America and the nearby Caribbean islands, periodically attacked the new rivals.

The main causes of the disaster, however, were two mosquito-borne illnesses: malaria and yellow fever (along with dysentery, a disease not carried by mosquitoes). Records kept by the colonists report dozens of deaths each week. The first time Spain assaulted New Edinburgh, its soldiers found four hundred fresh graves. They had been filled by victims of diseases that had come to the Americas from Europe and Africa.

Back in Scotland, the calamity of New Edinburgh set off riots. Much of the country's capital—that is, its cash available for investment—had been wiped out. At the time, England and Scotland were separate countries, although they shared a monarch. England, the bigger partner, had been pushing for a complete union for decades. Scots had resisted, fearing they would become a minor afterthought in an economy dominated by London. Now, as part of a union agreement, England promised to repay the people who had invested in New Edinburgh. The result was the formation of Great Britain— "with assistance from the fevers of Panama," in the words of historian J. R. McNeill in his book *Mosquito Empires*.

THE SUFFERING OF SUKEY CARTER

LANDON CARTER HAD A PROSPEROUS VIRGINIA
plantation about sixty miles north of Jamestown.
He was a devoted father who agonized as malaria
repeatedly struck his family in the summer
and fall of 1757. Worst affected was his infant
daughter, Sukey, who was racked by bouts of
chills and fever. Landon recorded her struggle in
a diary:

Dec. 7: Sukey looks badly all this evening with a
quick Pulse.

Dec. 8: 'Tis her usual Period of attack which
is now got to every Fortnight [two weeks]. . . .
Seems brisk and talkt cheerfully. Her fever not
higher.

Dec. 9: Continues better though very pale.

Dec. 10: Sukey a fever early and very sick at her

Mosquitos carried
both malaria and
yellow fever to the
Americas.

stomach and head ach. This fever went off in the night.

Dec. 11: The Child no fever today but I thought her pulse a little quick at night.

Dec. 12: Sukey's fever rose at 1 in the night. . . . This Child dangerous ill at 12, dead pale and blue. . . .

Dec. 13: Sukey's fever kept wearing away Yesterday till one in the night when she was quite clear.

To live in Virginia, a heartbroken Carter wrote, "it is necessary that a man should be acquainted with affliction, and 'tis certainly nothing short of it to be confined a whole year in tending one's sick children. Mine are now never well."

Sukey died the following April, just short of her third birthday.

As this nineteenth-century copy of an earlier drawing suggests, malaria was a constant fear in England's southeastern marshlands.

The Labor Question

Malaria had impacts beyond the suffering of its victims. It was a historical force that deformed cultures, pushing societies to answer questions in ways that now seem cruel and wrong. Consider the seventeenth-century English investors who wanted to make money in North America. Chesapeake Bay had no silver or gold. The best way to make a profit was to produce something else to export to the home country. In New England, the Pilgrims depended on selling beaver fur. In Chesapeake Bay, the English settled on tobacco, for which there was a huge demand.

To satisfy the demand for tobacco, the colonists wanted to expand the plantation area. To do that, they would have to cut down huge trees with hand tools; break up soil under the hot sun; hoe, water, and tend the growing tobacco plants; cut the heavy, sticky leaves and drape them on racks to dry; and pack the dried leaves into barrels for shipping. All this would require a lot of labor. Where would the colonists get it?

They had two basic choices: indentured servants or slaves.

Indentured servants were contract laborers

drawn from England's throngs of unemployed people. Planters paid for the servants' costly voyage across the Atlantic. The servants paid for their tickets by working for the planters for a set period of time, usually four to seven years. After that, indentured servants were free to claim their own land in the Americas—and, when they could afford it, to bring over indentured servants of their own.

Slavery is harder to define, because it has existed in many forms. Its key feature, though, is that the owner acquires the right to force slaves to work, and slaves never gain the right to leave. They must work and obey until they die or are freed by their owners. Indentured servants are members of society, although at a low level, and they have some rights under the law. Slaves are not usually considered members of society. In America, slavery took a harsher form than anything seen before in Europe, Asia, or Africa: chattel slavery, a brutal system in which slaves were regarded purely as property and had few rights, or none.

During the last quarter of the seventeenth century, the English colonists in North America chose slaves over servants. England became the world's biggest slaver. This was a turnaround for a nation that had previously led Europe in opposing slavery. Although slavery had been common throughout Europe (including England) in medieval times, by the seventeenth century it had become rare in England. The decline of slavery was due partly to the fact that England was aswarm with unemployed laborers ready to do whatever work needed to be done. It was also due to English disgust and anger over the capture and enslavement of thousands of English people by Islamic pirates in North Africa. The English, in fact, were Europe's least likely candidates to become slave masters.

Indeed, the English colonies had first turned to indentured servants. During the first century of colonization, between a third and half of the Europeans who arrived in North America were indentured servants. Slaves were rare at first in the English colonies—Virginia had only three hundred of them in 1650. Between 1680 and 1700, though, the number of slaves suddenly exploded. Virginia's slave population rose in those years, from three thousand to more than sixteen thousand, and then kept rising. In the same period the number of indentured servants shrank dramatically. It was a turning point in world history, a time when English America became a slave society and England became the dominant player in the slave trade.

Why this turnaround? Historians and economists have offered various explanations.

One explanation starts with the English Civil War of the mid-seventeenth century. This disastrous conflict caused the country's population to fall by almost 10 percent between 1650 and 1680. As a result, there were fewer English workers, which meant that their wages went up. This would have meant that Virginia planters had to pay higher prices to lure English indentured servants across the Atlantic. At the same time, indentured servants who had finished their years of labor in the American colonies were establishing new plantations and seeking their own indentured servants. Increased demand for servants also lifted the price.

This argument doesn't explain why colonists chose African slaves as their alternative labor source. Planters could have found labor in Scotland and Ireland, where desperate poverty and the poor harvests of the Little Ice Age had driven many people to flee their homes. Gangs of Scottish refugees roamed the streets of London, begging for work and food. They would have been obvious candidates for labor in the colonies. Yet the colonists turned to captive Africans—people who did not speak the language of the colonists, had no wish to cooperate, and cost more to transport across the sea than indentured servants. Why?

The fate of New Edinburgh suggests one answer. The calamity of that colony showed that Scots and other Europeans died too fast in malarial areas to be useful as forced labor. Individual English and Scottish people and their families continued to make their way to the Americas, but businesspeople turned against the idea of sending over large groups of Europeans. Instead they looked for alternative sources of labor. Alas, they found them.

Indians were one obvious source of labor in the colonies. South of Virginia, the colony of Carolina was founded in 1670 as a business venture and settled by two hundred English colonists from the Caribbean island colony of Barbados. The colonists supplied themselves with Indian slaves, obtaining them from other Indians. Slavery occurred in most native societies in the Americas, but it took different forms from place to place. Among the Powhatan of the Chesapeake Bay, for example, slavery was usually a temporary state. Slaves were prisoners of war who were treated as servants until they were killed, ransomed back to their original groups, or introduced into Powhatan society as full members.

Among many Indian societies south of Chesapeake Bay, war captives also became slaves, but slavery there was more common and longer lasting. When foreigners appeared in Carolina, Indians there were more than willing to trade their extra captives for axes, knives, metal pots, and, above all, guns. There was a political dimension, too. The leaders of the Carolina colony asked nearby native groups to provide them with slaves by raiding the tribes who had sided with Spain and France, the colonial powers that were rivals of the English.

For its first four decades, Carolina was a slave exporter—the place from which captive Indians were sent to the Caribbean, Virginia, New York, and Massachusetts. Yet although the Indian slave trade was profitable, it was very short-lived. By 1715 it had almost vanished. In part, the Indian slave trade was a victim of its own success. As Carolina's plantation owners requested more and more slave raids, the region became engulfed in warfare. Tribal groups that had suffered slave raids got hold of guns and attacked Carolina in a series of wars that the colony barely survived. Indian slaves who worked together in groups proved to be unreliable, even dangerous employees who used their knowledge of the land against their owners. Colonial records are full of accounts of the crimes committed by captive Indian laborers against their masters. Rhode Island and other northern colonies banned the import of the Indian slaves.

The worst problem, though, was disease. At first the English had praised Carolina's healthful climate. Yet malaria arrived in Carolina, as it had in Virginia. The Carolina colonists decided to grow rice. Soon after came reports of chills and fevers—probably because the paddies or flooded fields used for growing rice are notorious mosquito havens. Malaria was followed a few years later by yellow fever. Cemeteries quickly filled. Unfortunately, Indians were just as prone to malaria as English indentured servants. In addition, they were more vulnerable to other new diseases, such as smallpox.

Native people died in ghastly numbers across the entire Southeast. Struck by disease and slave raids, the Chickasaw lost almost half their population between 1685 and 1715. Some groups vanished completely. The colonists looked for a different solution to their labor needs. They wanted a labor force that was not vulnerable to disease. English servants and Indian slaves were out. Whom else could they try?

African Resistance

Anyone who lives through a bout of malaria gains immunity to the disease, in the same way that children who survive a bout of chickenpox or measles become immune to those diseases. Yet acquired immunity to malaria is only partial. Both *P. vivax* and *P. falciparum* malaria occur in different strains, or varieties. People who survive a particular strain of *P. vivax* or *P. falciparum* malaria become immune only to that strain (or strains very similar to it). A different strain can lay them low. The only way to get widespread immunity to malaria is to get sick repeatedly with different strains.

Inherited immunity is different. Someone with inherited immunity is born with a genetic makeup that resists infection by malaria. Often they have small mutations that change the surface or shape of their red blood cells in ways that block malaria parasites from climbing inside the cells. Inherited malaria resistance occurs in many parts of the world, but the peoples of West and Central Africa have more of it than anyone else. They are almost completely immune to *P. vivax* malaria and also have considerable resistance to *P. falciparum*. In addition, many people in those regions are repeatedly exposed to malaria during childhood. Survivors possess both types of immunity, inherited and acquired. When the English colonists in North America were struggling to meet their labor needs, adults in West and Central Africa were less vulnerable to malaria than anyone else on earth—as they still are.

Almost all the slaves ferried to the Americas came from West and Central Africa. *P. vivax* malaria could have come to North America with colonists from England, but *P. falciparum* never thrived in England. It almost certainly came to North America inside the bodies of African slaves. Yet with their inherited and acquired immunity, Africans were more likely to survive and produce children than the English colonists in malaria-ridden Virginia and Carolina. Biologically speaking, the Africans were fitter, which is another way of saying that, in those places, they were genetically superior. Rather than gaining an edge from this superiority, however, Africans saw their biological advantage turned against them. Their immunity became a reason for their enslavement.

Exact figures and causes for European and African deaths in the colonies are hard to pin down. Overall, though, it appears that in zones where *P. falciparum* malaria and yellow fever occurred, the English were between three and ten times more likely to die during their first year in America than Africans were. For European colonists, the economic logic was hard to ignore. If they wanted to grow tobacco, rice, or sugar, they were better off using African slaves than European indentured servants or Indian slaves.

Slavery and *P. falciparum* thrived together.

Consider the border between the states Pennsylvania and Maryland. Surveyed by Charles Mason and Jeremiah Dixon in 1768, this border became known as the Mason-Dixon Line. As a cultural boundary between North and South, between Yankee and Dixie, the Mason-Dixon Line marks one of the most lasting divisions in American culture. It roughly split the East Coast into two zones. South of the Mason-Dixon Line, *P. falciparum* was an endemic threat. North of the line, it was not, because temperatures were too cool for it to survive. South of the line, African slavery became a dominant institution. North of the line, it did not.

Malaria did not *cause* slavery, but it strengthened the economic case for it. Tobacco planters did not plot to take advantage of Africans' immunity to malaria. In fact, there is little evidence that the first slave owners understood malaria resistance, partly because they did not know what the disease really was and partly because people in isolated plantations could not easily make overall comparisons. Regardless of what they understood, though, planters who imported slaves tended to have an economic edge over planters who imported indentured servants. The slaves were more likely to survive and work for their owners. The indentured servants were more likely to die and be an economic loss. Successful planters imported more slaves, and newcomers copied the practices of their more successful neighbors. The slave trade took off.

Slavery would have existed in the Americas without the malaria parasite. In 1641, Massachusetts, which had little malaria, became the first colony to pass a law legalizing slavery. A century later, during the middle of the eighteenth century, the healthiest spot in English North America might have been the Connecticut River Valley in western Massachusetts. Malaria was almost nonexistent there. Infectious disease was extremely rare by the standards of the time. Yet slavery was part of the furniture of daily life. Almost every minister, usually the most important man in town, had one or two slaves. In Deerfield, one of the biggest villages in the valley, 8 percent of the people along the main street were slaves.

Far to the south, on the other side of the tropical malaria belt, was Argentina, which started as a Spanish colony in South America. With few mosquitoes and cool weather, Argentina had little malaria. Yet, like Massachusetts, it had African slaves. Between 1536, when Spain founded its first settlement in Argentina, and 1853, when Argentina abolished slavery, between 220,000 and 330,000 Africans landed in Buenos Aires, the main port and capital of Argentina.

North of Argentina was Brazil, which had been colonized by Portugal. It was closer to the equator and therefore warmer. Mosquitoes and malaria both thrived in Brazil. So did slavery. Many more slaves arrived there than in Argentina, as many as 2.2 million. By the 1760s and 1770s, about half the people in both Brazil and Argentina were of African descent. In spite of this similarity, the impact of slavery in the two countries was completely different. Slavery was never vital to colonial Argentina's most important industries, such as cattle ranching. Colonial Brazil, in contrast, could not have functioned without slaves, which were essential to its most important industry: sugar. Argentina was a society with slaves. Brazil was culturally and economically *defined by* slavery.

All American colonies had slaves. Yet the colonies to which the Columbian Exchange brought *P. falciparum* malaria ended up with more slaves. They became slave societies in ways that other colonies did not.

Yellow Jack

In the 1640s a few Dutch refugees from Brazil landed on Barbados, the easternmost Caribbean island. Unlike the rest of the Caribbean, Barbados never had a large Indian population. English colonists had moved in hoping to cash in on the tobacco boom. When the Dutch arrived, the island had about six thousand inhabitants, including two thousand indentured servants and two hundred slaves.

Tobacco turned out not to grow particularly well on Barbados—but there was an alternative. The Dutch refugees had learned in Brazil how to plant sugarcane, and they shared this knowledge with the English colonists on Barbados. Sugar was in demand to satisfy Europe's sweet tooth, and Barbados proved to be good sugarcane territory. Production of sugar rapidly grew.

Sugar production was hard work that required many hands. Sugarcane is a tall, tough Asian grass, somewhat like its cousin bamboo. Plantations burned the crop before harvesting it to prevent the knifelike leaves from slashing workers. Swinging long knives into the hard, soot-smeared cane under the tropical sun, field hands quickly spattered themselves with a sticky mixture of dust, ash, and cane juice. The cut stalks were crushed in a mill to squeeze out their juice, which was boiled down in great kettles enveloped in smoke and steam. Workers ladled the hot syrup into clay pots. As the syrup cooled, crystals of pure sugar formed. What remained in liquid form was molasses. Most of the molasses was used to produce the alcoholic drink rum, which required feeding yet another fire under another infernal cauldron.

Where would the Barbados cane planters get the labor they needed? In Virginia, slaves cost twice as much as indentured servants, if not more. Yet the Dutch West India Company, a badly run outfit that was desperate for cash, was willing to sell Africans cheaply in Barbados. Slaves and servants there were roughly the same price. The island's new sugar barons imported servants and slaves by the thousands: beggars and the unemployed from England, luckless captives from wars in Africa. Covered in sweat and gummy cane soot, Europeans and Africans wielded their knives side by side in the cane fields.

Then the Columbian Exchange raised the cost of indentured servants.

Hidden on the slave ships was a stowaway from Africa: the mosquito *Aedes aegypti*. Inside its gut it carried its own hidden stowaway, the virus that causes yellow fever, a disease that originated in Africa. The yellow fever virus spends most of its life cycle inside the mosquito. It uses human beings only to pass from one insect to the next. Typically it remains in a human host less than two weeks. During this time it drills into huge numbers of cells and hijacks their genetic material to make billions of copies of itself. These flood the bloodstream. Biting mosquitoes pick them up and pass them to new hosts.

The cellular invasion of yellow fever usually has little effect on children. Adults, though, are hit by massive internal bleeding. Blood collects and thickens in the stomach. Sufferers vomit up the black blood—the chief symptom of yellow fever. Another symptom is jaundice, or a yellowing of the skin, which gave rise to the disease's nickname of yellow jack. (A "Yellow Jack" was a flag flown by ships that were quarantined, or unable to land, because of disease on board.) The virus kills about half its adult victims. Survivors acquire lifelong immunity. In Africa, yellow fever was a childhood disease that caused relatively little suffering and made many people immune. In the Caribbean, it was a dire plague that passed over Africans while ravaging Europeans, Indians, and black slaves who had been born on the islands.

The initial yellow fever onslaught began in 1647 and lasted five years. It hit first in Barbados. Terror spread as far away as Massachusetts, which quarantined incoming ships for the first time. One record from the period says that six thousand people died on Barbados alone. Almost all the victims were Europeans—a searing blow for the island's colonists. A modern researcher estimates that the epidemic may have killed 20 to 50 percent of the people living in the Caribbean, Central America, and Florida. Most of the victims were European or Indian.

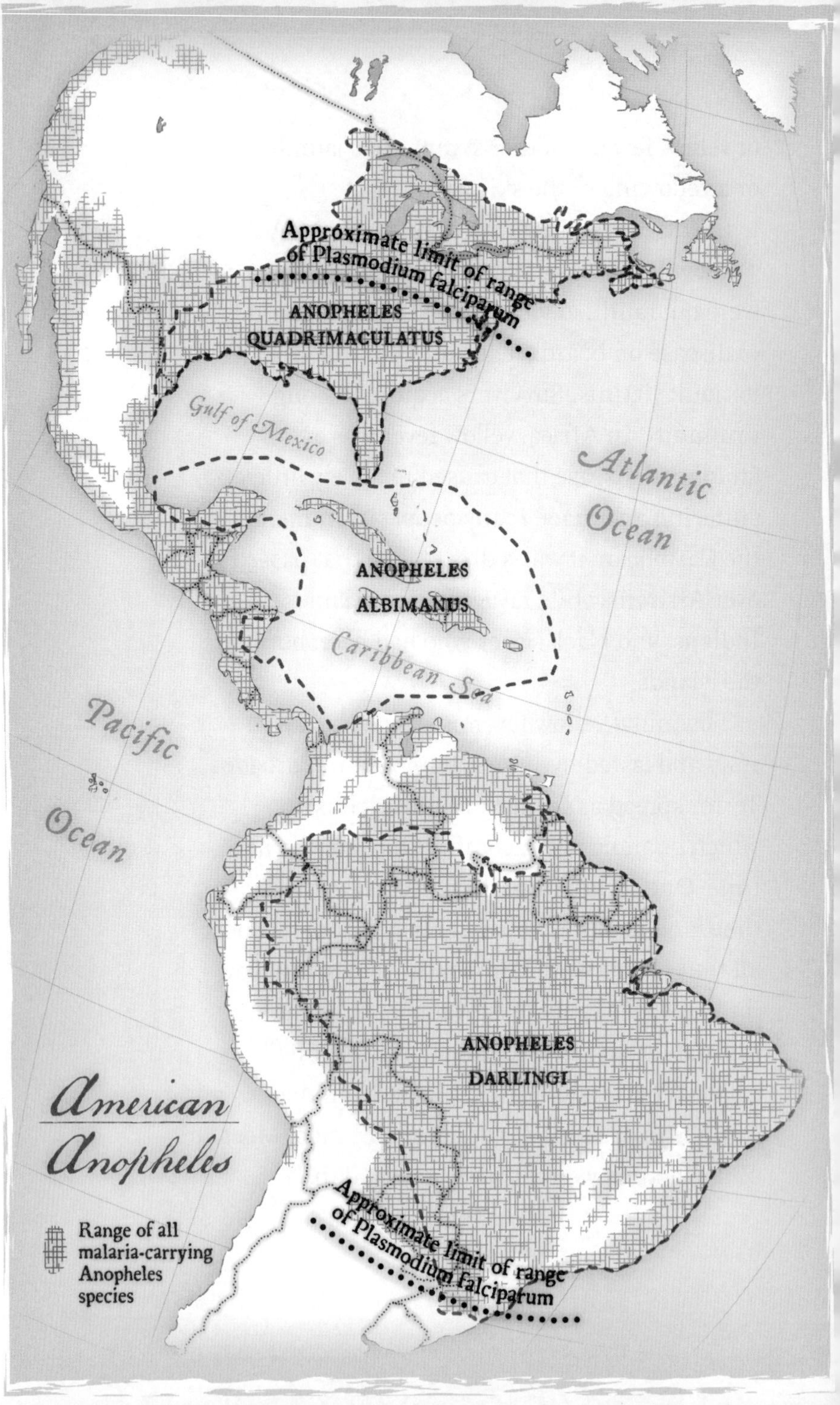

Approximate limit of range
of Plasmodium falciparum

ANOPHELES
QUADRIMACULATUS

Gulf of Mexico

*Atlantic
Ocean*

ANOPHELES

ALBIMANUS

Caribbean Sea

Pacific

Ocean

ANOPHELES

DARLINGI

*American
Anopheles*

Range of all
malaria-carrying
Anopheles
species

Approximate limit of range
of Plasmodium falciparum

The epidemic didn't wipe out the sugar industry. Sugar was too profitable. Barbados, an island of just 166 square miles, was already making more money than the rest of English North America. Sugar had spread to other Caribbean islands, and slave labor along with it.

The new diseases also spread through the warm regions of the Americas. Malaria traveled from the Caribbean to South America, then up the Amazon River, where there were many *Anopheles* mosquito species available to carry the parasite. The first Europeans to visit Amazonia described it as a thriving, healthful place. That was before malaria—and, later, yellow fever— turned many of the region's rivers into death traps. By 1782, malaria was sabotaging European expeditions in the upper reaches of the river basin.

The effects of disease were even worse in the northeastern bulge of South America, a region that geographer Susanna Hecht has called the Caribbean Amazon. Bounded to the south by the Amazon River in Brazil and to the west by the Orinoco River in Venezuela, this region was a watery place that the native Arawak and Carib people controlled with sprawling networks of

dikes, dams, and canals. They managed large areas of forest for tree crops, especially the palms that in tropical places provide fruit, oil, starch, wine, and building material.

This landscape of gardens, orchards, and waterways served for centuries as a gateway between the islands of the Caribbean and the interior of South America. By the eighteenth century, however, diseases brought by the Columbian Exchange had weakened the local people. Smallpox, influenza, and tuberculosis cleared the way for malaria and then yellow fever. Indians retreated into the interior. Europeans seized the coast, creating sugar plantations.

Part of the coast became the French colony of Guyane (now known as French Guiana), site of the notorious prison called Devil's Island. As many as eighty thousand Frenchmen were sent to Guyane in the nineteenth and early twentieth centuries, either to Devil's Island or to labor in chain gangs on plantations on the mainland. Very, very few of them returned to France. Malaria either killed prisoners or weakened them so that they fell victim to other ailments. Disease claimed so many that Guyane became

(left)
After visiting the prison islands of France's Guyane Colony in the 1860s, an artist recorded the sea burial of a convict, probably a victim of malaria or yellow fever.

known as a "dry guillotine." The guillotine, an execution machine invented in France, chopped off victims' heads with a sharp, sliding blade. Malaria was a blade that killed without needing to wet itself with blood.

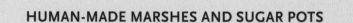

HUMAN-MADE MARSHES AND SUGAR POTS

WITH THE SUCCESS OF SUGAR PLANTING IN Barbados, colonists from England, France, the Netherlands, Portugal, and Spain began clearing neighboring Caribbean islands as fast as possible, planting cane in the flatlands and cutting trees on the hills for fuel. With the trees gone, the soil began to erode. Rainfall, no longer absorbed by forests, washed soil down the slopes and formed coastal marshes. In the not-too-distant future, workers would be ordered to carry the soil in baskets back up the slopes in an attempt to reverse the damage.

Even the worst ecological mismanagement benefits some species. One of the winners in the Caribbean was *Anopheles albimanus*, a mosquito species that became the region's chief carrier of

Sugar plantations stripped Barbados bare, as shown in the background of this photograph of workers' huts in the 1890s.

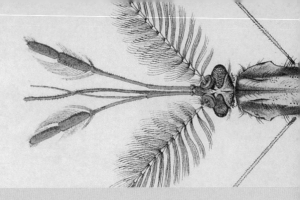

malaria. This mosquito likes to breed in coastal, algae-covered marshes. Deforestation and erosion are its friends. It can reproduce in huge numbers when conditions are right.

From the point of view of *A. albimanus*, the arrival of Europeans in the Caribbean was the start of a golden age. The Europeans created new coastal marshes where the mosquito population soared. The species gradually grew accustomed to hosting the *P. vivax* malaria parasite, and it spread *P. vivax* from the Caribbean to Mexico. *P. falciparum* did not arrive until much later, partly because the mosquito was more resistant to it.

The mosquito that carries yellow fever, *Aedes aegypti*, also benefited from human activity in the Caribbean. It likes to breed in small amounts of water, near human beings.

Sugar mills in the Caribbean during the seventeenth and eighteenth centuries abounded with excellent breeding places: the crude clay pots into which boiled cane juice was poured to form sugar crystals. These pots would have been full of sugary material, food for the bacteria that mosquito larvae eat. Sugar plantations were like factories for producing yellow fever.

The Europeans who came to the islands did not know these biological details. However, they did know that the Caribbean was, as one historian of malaria put it, "a lethal environment" for anyone who was not immune to malaria and yellow fever. That gave Africans, many of whom were immune to those diseases, an advantage— one that helped doom them to slavery.

War and Mosquitoes

Disease has shaped history in many ways. One example is the role played by the malaria parasite in the birth of the United States.

In May of 1778, with the Revolutionary War in full swing, Henry Clinton became commander in chief of the British forces in the rebellious American colonies. The British believed that the Carolinas and Georgia were full of loyalists—that is, colonists who remained loyal to Great Britain. Based partly on inaccurate reports from loyalists who had fled to London, British leaders thought that these southern loyalists existed in large numbers but were afraid to declare their support of the home country. Clinton decided upon a "southern strategy": he would send a force south to hold the region long enough for the silent loyalist majority to declare its support for the British king.

Although Clinton didn't know it, he was leading an invasion of the malaria zone.

British troops were not seasoned—they had not endured and survived malaria attacks. Two-thirds of them were from malaria-free Scotland. The British soldiers who *had* served a year or two in the colonies had done so mostly in New York and New England, north of the malaria zone. By contrast, the southern

colonists were seasoned. Almost all were immune to
P. vivax, and many had survived *P. falciparum*.

British troops successfully besieged Charleston,
South Carolina, in 1780. A month later Clinton
left for the North, instructing his troops to chase
the Americans into the backcountry. He put
Major General Charles Cornwallis in charge of
this mission. Cornwallis marched inland in June,
the prime season for the *Anopheles* mosquito. By
autumn, he complained, disease had "nearly ruined"
his army. So many men were sick that the British
could barely fight. Loyalist troops from the colonies
were the only men able to march. Cornwallis
himself lay ill while his men lost the Battle of King's
Mountain. In the words of malaria historian J. R.
McNeill, "Cornwallis's army simply melted away."

Beaten back by disease, Cornwallis abandoned
the Carolinas and marched to Chesapeake
Bay, where he planned to join another British
force. He arrived in June 1781. Clinton ordered
him to take a position on the coast so that the
army could be carried by ship to New York if
necessary. Cornwallis protested that Chesapeake
Bay was notoriously disease-ridden. It didn't
matter. He had to be on the coast if he was to
be useful. So his army marched to Yorktown,

fifteen miles from Jamestown, and camped between two marshes, near some rice fields. Cornwallis bitterly described the location as "some acres of an unhealthy swamp."

To his horror and surprise, a French fleet appeared off Chesapeake Bay, ending the possibility of escape by sea and trapping the British. Meanwhile, General George Washington marched his Revolutionary Army south from New York. By this time the American Revolution was so short of money and supplies that Washington's men had mutinied twice—but an opportunity had arisen. The British army was unable to move and was stricken by disease. Cornwallis later estimated that only 3,800 of his 7,700 men were fit to fight.

The bravery and skill of the revolution's leaders contributed to the victory of the American colonists over the British. Yet what McNeill called "revolutionary mosquitoes" played an equally vital role. With Cornwallis's troops falling in ever-greater numbers to the diseases of the Columbian Exchange, the British army surrendered on October 17, 1781, and the United States was born.

Although almost forgotten today, yellow fever was a terror from the U.S. south to Argentina until the 1930s, when a safe vaccine was developed. This drawing illustrated an article about an 1873 outbreak in Florida.

To celebrate the 2010 Olympics, China displayed this copy of Zheng He's flagship. Six centuries after the original was built, the ship still was large enough to astonish crowds.

PART THREE

PACIFIC JOURNEYS

ATLANTIC CROSSINGS WERE ONLY THE FIRST half of the Columbian Exchange. Voyages across the Pacific completed the interconnection of the world. Cities such as Potosí, in South America; Manila, in the Philippines; and Yuegang, in southeast China, became bustling, essential links in an economic exchange that knit the world together. Along the way, the exchange brought sweet potatoes and corn to China—with accidental, devastating effects on Chinese ecosystems. Those effects, in turn, shaped economic and political developments. Carried across the sea as part of the Columbian Exchange, sweet potatoes and corn played a major part in the rise and fall of China's last imperial dynasty, and in the history of the Communist state that came afterward and that still rules the country.

CHAPTER 5

SHIPLOADS OF SILVER

VAST, SPLENDID FLEETS OF SHIPS SAILED FORTH
from China between 1405 and 1433. Ordered
by the emperor of the Ming dynasty, and
commanded by an admiral named Zheng He,
the fleets passed among the islands and along
the coasts of Southeast Asia. They crossed the
Indian Ocean all the way to southern Africa.
Enormous wide-bellied ships by the hundreds,
encrusted with precious metals, banners
snapping atop their forests of masts—the fleets
inspired wonder and also scared the wits out of
every foreign leader who saw them.

Zheng's ships featured new technical
developments that European shipbuilders would
not discover for a century, including rust-proof
nails and watertight compartments. His flagship
was more than three hundred feet long and one

PART THREE: PACIFIC JOURNEYS

hundred fifty feet wide, the biggest wooden vessel ever built. His grandest expedition had 317 ships, more than twice as many as the Spanish Armada, which was the largest European fleet up to that time. Yet Zheng He's voyages became a target in the political infighting of the Chinese court. One faction supported them; a rival faction opposed them. The emperor's son and successor sided with the group that opposed the voyages. He ended the grand naval ventures the day he took the imperial throne. China didn't again send ships so far outside its borders until the nineteenth century.

China could have continued its voyages. It could easily have sent a fleet around Africa and north to Europe. Why didn't it?

Some modern scholars have seen China's failure to continue its sea voyages as a sign that Chinese society was fatally turned in on itself, lacking in curiosity and drive, determined to keep itself apart from the rest of the world. They have painted a picture of imperial China as static and unchanging, "a reluctant improver and a bad learner," in the words of one historian. Others, though, argue that Zheng He never encountered a nation richer or more advanced than his own.

Technologically speaking, China was so far ahead of the rest of Eurasia that foreign lands had little to offer except raw materials, which China could get without the expense and trouble of sending gigantic fleets on long journeys. According to political scientist Jack Goldstone of George Mason University, the Chinese empire stopped long-range exploration "for the same reason the United States stopped sending men to the moon—there was nothing there to justify the costs of such voyages."

Whatever the reasons for starting the sea ventures and then stopping them, Zheng He's voyages were a break in China's history. During most of the Ming dynasty, which lasted from 1368 to 1644, China's rulers banned private sea trade. The emperors did conduct their own trade; they just wouldn't let others do it, too. A few rulers opened up trade, but they were exceptions. As a rule, the Ming dynasty clamped down on international exploration and trade. The ban was so strict that in 1525 the royal court ordered coastal officials to destroy all private seagoing vessels.

Fifty years later, a new emperor changed course once again. With the reluctant blessing of the imperial court, a new generation of Chinese ships went on the waters. Soon the Ming dynasty had been drawn into a worldwide network of exchange. The Chinese economy became enmeshed with Europe (a place China had previously seen as too poor to be worth bothering with) and the Americas (a place the emperors hadn't known existed).

Why did China lower its barriers to trade and let in this flood of change? One reason was political: the desire of the Ming to strengthen the power of the imperial government by increasing the income it gained from trade. Another reason was economic: China had severe money woes. The empire had lost control of its own coinage. Merchants were buying and selling goods with little lumps of silver. China desperately needed more silver. To get that silver, it lifted its trade ban and opened itself to the world. Soon the great ships of Spain's galleon trade were carrying silver to China and returning with silk. These were the final links in the global economic and ecological network begun by Columbus in the Caribbean and by Legazpi in the Philippines.

The Ming court had long feared that open trade would lead to chaos. Trade did have catastrophic effects on China, although not the ones imperial officials predicted. As the Columbian Exchange reached across the Pacific, it first took economic form: trade and money, and their effects on politics. Later would come the ecological exchange, with dire consequences for China.

Pirates and Merchants

While China's bans on foreign trade were in place, they did not stop all foreign contact. Foreigners were allowed to stay in certain government residences and to offer gifts to the throne, called "tribute payments." Then the emperor would, out of politeness, give them Chinese goods in return. He also allowed them to sell any of their gifts that he didn't want, which was often quite a lot. In 1403–1404, at the height of the supposed ban on foreign merchants, the Ming court hosted "tribute delegations" from no fewer than thirty-eight nations.

Merchants along the Chinese coast recognized this system for what it was: a way for the government to control international commerce. The Ming wanted the profits from trade, but not the foreign traders themselves. With few exceptions, all contact with the outside world was supposed to be supervised by government officials in Beijing, the capital. The court reasoned that because oceangoing trade was outlawed, the nation did not need a navy to police such trade. China reduced its navy to a few vessels, not enough to patrol the nation's long coastline. The unsurprising result was a dizzying outbreak of smuggling, or illegal commerce.

Wokou swarmed on the southeastern coast. The Chinese term means "Japanese pirates," but most weren't Japanese and many were smugglers rather than true pirates. The majority of *wokou* groups were led by Chinese traders. Their ships were crewed by a crazy quilt of citizens in trouble: scholars who had failed to get government jobs, bankrupt businesspeople, draft dodgers who had fled rather than perform required military service, fired clerks, starving farmers, disgraced monks, escaped convicts, and of course actual professional smugglers. Scattered among them were a few skilled sailors lured into piracy by the promise of wealth. When

Ming-era Fujian

ZHEJIANG

JIANGXI

FUJIAN

Fuzhou

East China Sea

Quanzhou

Amoy (Xiamen)

Yongding

Yuegang

Zhangpu

GULANGYU ISLAND

WU ISLAND

TAIWAN

GUANGDONG

River

Jiulong

officials tried to stop these people, violence followed. Every now and then the *wokou* took over a city. The merchant-pirates would trade peacefully if they could, not so peacefully if they couldn't.

China's efforts to control piracy were hampered by a string of incompetent emperors. Worst affected by piracy was Fujian, a poor province on the southeastern coast that couldn't grow enough food to feed itself. Half of Fujian's rice had to be imported—not easy, because Fujian is separated from the rest of China by mountains. The province does, however, have fine harbors along its stony coast. Fujian depended on the sea, and when international trade was officially banned, the Fujianese found themselves in an uncomfortable position.

In 1547 a pirate-smuggler-merchant group of Spanish, Portuguese, and Dutch hustlers set up a base on Wu Island, near the Fujianese port city Yuegang. Chinese and Japanese *wokou* happily sent ships to trade with them. So did businesspeople from Yuegang. A busy, multilingual market sprang up in Wu Island's harbor. Zhu Wan, the governor of Fujian, sent soldiers to drive out the foreigners. The

(top left)
The walled city of Yuegang, shown in a seventeenth-century Chinese map, was once one of the world's most important ports.

(bottom left)
A former pirate stronghold, Wu Island, in the hazy waters off Yuegang, is now a center for fishing and aquaculture.

merchant-pirate group held the soldiers off, so
the governor, as an example to others, beheaded
ninety Fujianese merchants who had traded at
Wu Island. Without local merchants willing to
trade with them, the foreigners abandoned the
island and gave up their attempt to trade openly.

Zhu Wan was not satisfied. He assaulted
another major smuggling base and sank more
than twelve hundred illegal vessels. A *wokou*
leader known as "Baldy" Li led followers by the
hundreds to a new base in southern Fujian.
Zhu's men hunted them down, killing some
and capturing others. Many of Li's gang turned
out to be from important merchant families in
Yuegang. Angered by this evidence of illegal
ties between leading local families and foreign
smugglers, Zhu executed his captives.

The executions united Zhu's enemies
against him. The wealthy families of Yuegang
complained to the emperor. Zhu found
himself demoted, then fired, and then under
investigation. He killed himself with poison in
1550. Made bold by his absence, pirate gangs
seized entire towns and ran wild. In one city
north of Yuegang, twenty thousand people
died after a pirate assault. The *wokou* terrorized

the region. Yet even as they attacked Yuegang, twenty-four of the city's merchants pooled their resources and built a fleet to work with the pirates in an interconnecting business network. The merchants had access to markets within China. The smugglers had access to foreign goods to sell to those markets. Business boomed.

Soon other, similar networks sprang up. The region became a violent, bewildering tangle of overlapping loyalties and betrayals, as business gangs and pirate gangs fought over the smuggling trade. Local officials were powerless to put an end to the trade or the violence. The world's richest, most technologically advanced nation had lost control of its borders. In 1567 a new Ming emperor gave in and lifted the ban on private trade.

Yet the Chinese government did not change course simply because it could not stop the smuggling. It had come to realize how desperately Beijing needed the most important thing that the merchants had to offer: silver. China needed silver so badly because its money supply was in terrible shape, and had been that way for a long time.

Out of Money

Several hundred years before the birth of Christ,
the Chinese government began to issue round
coins made of bronze, a blend of copper and
tin. Each coin had a square hole in its center.
Bronze was not especially valuable, and the coins
weren't worth much. To create units of larger
value, people strung the bronze coins together
into groups of a hundred or a thousand. The
strings were heavy, bulky, and still not worth
much. Asking large-scale Chinese traders to use
them was like asking today's big bankers to buy
whole companies with rolls of quarters. Worse,
the Chinese government did not have enough
copper to keep up with the demand for coins.

Starting in 1161, the imperial government
issued paper currency. It printed various
denominations of banknotes called *huizi*, worth
between two hundred and three thousand
bronze coins. (The first European banknotes
appeared in 1661, five centuries later.) The
banknotes and bronze coins were examples of
two different kinds of money: *fiat* money and
commodity money. Fiat money, such as the *huizi*
or today's U.S. dollar and European euro, has
no value in itself. It is worth something only

because a government says it is. Commodity money, such as China's bronze coins or the silver pesos that circulated in the Spanish Empire, has value because it is made of a substance that is worth something in its own right—even if its value is not high, as in the case of the bronze Chinese coins.

With commodity money, governments cannot completely control the money supply. The currency is at the risk of random shocks, such as a sudden shortage or surplus of whatever the money is made of, which may change its value. If silver becomes scarce, for example, its price may rise so much that the silver in a coin becomes more valuable than the denomination of the coin itself. People begin melting down the coins, leading to a shortage of money.

With fiat money, in contrast, the government has near-complete control over the money supply. It decides how many banknotes are needed, and it controls the mints that produce them. This is also a weakness, however, because governments can print so much money that the economy is flooded with banknotes. When this happens, the purchasing power of the money goes down, and the price of goods and services goes up—a process known as inflation. Runaway inflation can make a currency practically worthless. Before the Ming dynasty came to power in China, two earlier dynasties had suffered from high inflation of their paper money.

The first Ming emperor ordered that new bronze coins be issued in his name—no more worthless paper bills! Unfortunately, he discovered that the empire had nearly exhausted its copper mines. Because copper was scarce, its price rose so high that the coins cost more to make than they were supposed to be worth. It was as if every penny cost two pennies to manufacture. For this reason not many coins were issued. Ming coins were so rare, in fact, that businesspeople did not want to accept them. Merchants had too little experience with the new coins to know whether they were genuine or counterfeit. Yet China needed new money. What could be done?

Once again the government turned to the printing presses and issued paper money—and once again, inflation exploded. The value of the new banknotes dropped by 75 percent in just ten years. At the same time, the value of old, pre-Ming coins (which people trusted and understood) increased. So did the practice of counterfeiting, or manufacturing fake coins. Businesspeople were so desperate for some way for their customers to pay them that they accepted the counterfeits anyway, although they charged more for their use. As people snatched up all the old and counterfeit coins they could find, the value of paper bills continued to fall.

In an attempt to gain control of the nation's currency, the Ming dynasty periodically outlawed the use of coins, hoping to force people to use the paper bills. Each time, the ban failed, and the government would again allow coins to circulate—until the next ban. Meanwhile, the Ming kept printing paper money, fueling inflation. The nation's currency had become unpredictable. Each new emperor produced coins with his name stamped on the face. When he died, his successor would quickly declare that the last emperor's coins were worthless and that only coins minted by the new emperor could be used as currency. Merchants could see their entire wealth wiped out in a single day by the death of an emperor.

Silver had long been seen as a commodity of value, too rare and costly to be used for ordinary,

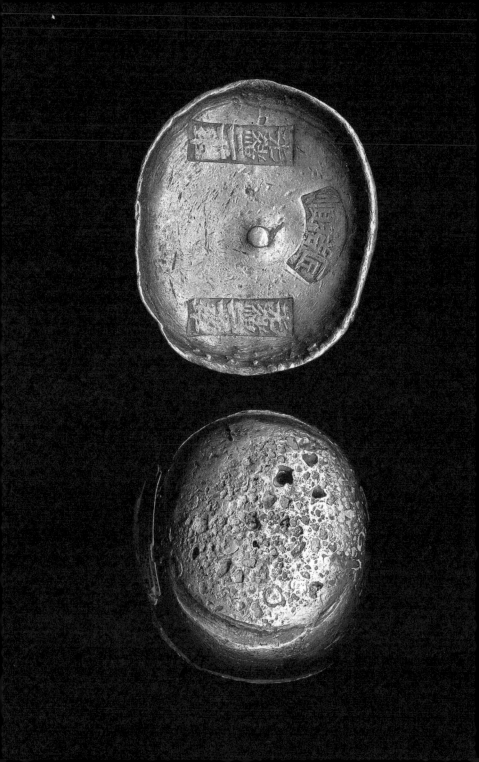

small-scale businesses. Yet the uncertainty over bronze coins and paper money reached the point where merchants took to carrying around little silver ingots, or pieces of metal. When traders met, they used these ingots to buy and sell, weighing them with jeweler's scales and clipping off needed sums with special shears. Awkward as it was, this system was better than using coins that might lose their value at any time. One writer complained in 1570 that everyone was paying bills with splinters of silver. Grudgingly and gradually the Ming emperors adopted the silver system, too. Beijing ordered citizens to pay more and more of their taxes in silver instead of turning over a portion of their harvest, as had been done for eight hundred years. By the 1570s, more than 90 percent of the taxes collected by Beijing arrived as lumps of shiny metal. There was just one problem.

China was the world's biggest economy. The "silverization" of that economy meant that tens of millions of wealthy Chinese needed chunks of silver to pay taxes and run businesses. Demand for silver soared. Inconveniently, China's silver mines were just as played out as its copper mines. People had trouble laying their hands

(left)
These small silver ingots were used in the Ming and Qing eras instead of coins.

153

on enough silver to pay for anything, including taxes. The only close source of silver was Japan, but China and Japan were not friendly. (They would soon fight a war in Korea.) So, to get the silver they needed, China's merchants turned to *wokou*. They sold silk and porcelain to brutal men for silver, and then turned around and used the silver to pay their taxes, which in turn paid for military campaigns against the brutal men. The Ming government was at war with its own money supply.

Then Beijing finally allowed the merchants of Fujian to trade overseas without fear of punishment. The merchants sent thousands of people throughout Asia to establish trading posts. Even a backwater such as the village of Manila in the Philippines might have had as many as one hundred fifty Chinese residents in 1571, when the Spanish adventurer Legazpi arrived (as described in chapter 1). Hundreds more Chinese lived in other parts of the Philippines. The unexpected discovery of silver-bearing Spaniards from the Americas in the Philippines was, from the Chinese point of view, a miracle. The galleons that carried Spanish silver were ships full of money.

"The Treasure of the World"

How did the silver get onto those galleons?
Stories say that it began with a man looking for
a lost llama in 1545. The llama, a relative of the
camel, is one of the few animals comfortable
at thirteen thousand feet above sea level on a
plateau in the Andes Mountains, at the southern
tip of Bolivia. On a bare, dome-shaped hill
clawed by wind and snow and surrounded by
taller mountains splashed with ice, the man
stumbled. He steadied himself by seizing a
shrub, which came out of the shallow soil. In the
hole made by its roots the man saw a metallic
sparkle. As others would soon discover, the man
was standing on a ledge of silver three hundred
feet long, three hundred feet deep, and thirteen
feet wide—and he had just made the biggest
silver strike in history.

Typical silver ores contain at most a few
percent of silver. That ledge in the Andes was
as much as 20 percent silver. The discovery led
to a boomtown known formally as the Imperial
Village of Potosí. Two decades after the strike,
Potosí had a population of as much as fifty
thousand. It would have had even more if Spain
had not done everything in its power to keep

people out so that the government could control the exploitation of the riches. Despite these efforts, the population of Potosí grew to one hundred sixty thousand by 1611. The city was as big as London or Amsterdam. Cold, crowded, and violent, it was the highest, richest city in the world.

Lawless, luxurious Potosí set a pattern that many boomtowns later followed. Miners who had struck it rich gave fortunes to beggars and spent extravagant sums on swords and clothes. In one bidding war at a market stall, two men drove the price for a single fish to five thousand pesos, many years' income for most Europeans. At one celebration, a city street was paved with silver bars. "I am rich Potosí," boasted the city's coat of arms, "the treasure of the world, the king of the mountains, the envy of kings."

At first the Spaniards depended on the local Indians' knowledge of metalworking. Indians knew how to build low-temperature smelters, or ovens, that purified the rich ore without boiling away the silver, a technique unknown to the Spaniards. Later, however, the Spaniards learned a method of using the liquid metal mercury to get silver from the ore. After seeing

(top left)
In a 1768 drawing, Potosí spreads across the plains below the silver mountains. Cold, crowded, and violent, it was the highest city in the world and probably the richest.

(bottom left)
The artist Theodorus de Bry never saw the mines of Potosí, but he captured something of their cruelty in this engraving from the 1590s.

a demonstration of this method, the Spanish governor of Peru and Bolivia seized control of a mountain eight hundred miles northwest of Potosí that had mercury deposits. A supply of mercury meant that the Spaniards no longer needed the Indians' smelters to purify their silver ore. They began treating the native people solely as a source of labor, forcing them to deliver a set number of men each week to the silver and mercury mines.

At the start, roughly four thousand Indians were set to work each week at each mountain. Mine owners also imported several hundred African slaves each year. Conditions in the mines were appalling and inhumane. Exposure to mercury, a slow-acting poison, crippled or killed so many people that some Indian parents maimed their children to protect them from having to serve in the mercury pits. At Potosí, Indians carried hundred-pound loads of ore up and down dangling rope-and-leather ladders in almost complete darkness. When miners hit a patch of low-quality ore, they were forced to work harder to make their quota of silver. Failure to meet the quota meant punishment by whips, clubs, and stones. "If twenty healthy Indians enter on Monday," wrote an outraged priest to the Spanish royal secretary, "half come out on Saturday as cripples." How, he asked, could Christian leaders allow this?

One reason the law broke down underground was that it had broken down on the surface. Violence of every kind flourished in Potosí. The permanent European population of the city consisted almost entirely of young men trying to make their fortunes. According to one chronicler at the time, "killing and hurting each other was the sole entertainment." Construction workers found murder victims stuffed into walls or shoved under rocks. City council members wore protective chain mail to meetings and carried swords and pistols. Political disputes were sometimes settled by duels fought right in the council meeting room.

Over time the city's violence changed from face-offs between individuals to full-fledged battles between gangs from different ethnic groups. One gang war pitted people from different parts of Spain against one another: Spaniards from the southeast fought Basques, who came from a mountainous region on Spain's northern coast, spoke their own language, and were culturally separate from Spain.

Incredibly, gang violence had almost no effect on the flow of silver. Even as Basques and Spaniards fought in the streets, they cooperated in mining and refining the silver, and then shipping it from Potosí. Shipping was a huge task. One account tells how a shipment of 7,771 silver bars left Potosí in 1549, four years after the lode was discovered. Each bar was about 99 percent silver and weighed about eighty pounds. All were stamped with serial numbers and marked by the owner, the tax man, and the assayer (who tested the purity of the metal). The bars were loaded onto llamas, three or four bars for each animal. The shipment required more than two thousand llamas, which were guarded by more than a thousand Indians, who were overseen by squads of armed Spaniards. Despite these obstacles, the Americas produced a river of silver. That silver flow would change the economy of the entire planet.

THE LLAMA.——*Auchenia Glama.*

THE LLAMA is generally about four feet and a half high, and nearly six feet in length. Its usual weight is about 300 pounds. It is a native of the Cordilleras of the Andes, and is still more frequently found in Peru and Chili. Llamas live together in herds of one hundred or two hundred each, and feed on a peculiar kind of grass or reed that covers the mountains on the sides of which they dwell. While they can procure green herbage, they are never known to drink. They are mild and tractable animals, and are used in many parts of South America to carry burdens. They were formerly employed in the ploughing of land. Like the Camel, they lie down to be loaded; and, when they are wearied with much labour, no blows will induce them to proceed. Although very gentle if well-used, the Llama easily takes offence at any insult, and then it has a bad habit of spitting at the person with whom it is angry. This animal slow and careful in moving when it is under control, or when loaded with baggage; but among it own native hills or valleys it has a swifter pace than an excellent horse.

PUBLISHED UNDER THE DIRECTION OF THE COMMITTEE OF GENERAL LITERATURE AND EDUCATION, APPOINTED BY THE SOCIETY FOR PROMOTING CHRISTIAN KNOWLEDGE.
PRICE ½d. PLAIN; 2d. COLOURED.
11.]
R. CLAY, PRINTER, BREAD STREET HILL.

(above)
One of the few animals comfortable high in the mountains, the llama helped carry silver to the galleon ships below. One llama could carry three or four bars of silver at about eighty pounds each.

(left)
Much of the silver from Potosí and Mexico was transformed into "cob" coins, hammered between crudely engraved dies. This coin was made in Potosí in the 1570s.

The Galleon Trade

Between the sixteenth century and the eighteenth century, more than one hundred fifty thousand tons of silver came out of mines in Spain's American colonies. It doubled or even tripled the world's supply of precious metals. Spanish silver washed around the planet, overwhelming governments and financial institutions such as banks. The Spanish silver peso became a universal currency, linking European nations much as the euro does today. Pesos were the main currency in the Portuguese, Dutch, and British empires, and they were widely used in France and the German states.

The money supply across Europe was silver, and the addition of a lot of new silver created an explosion in that money supply. This led to inflation and financial instability. After sixty years of frenzied silver production in the Americas, the world had so much silver that the metal's value began to fall. A million pesos in 1640 was worth about a third of what a million pesos had been worth in 1540.

As the price of silver slid downward, so did the profits from silver mining, the financial backbone of the Spanish empire. The king collected the same amount of taxes in silver as before, but silver's value plunged, throwing the government into crisis. Spain's economy turned to ash. Then, one after another, like a string of firecrackers, the economies of a dozen other countries that were equally dependent on Spanish silver blew up. The wealthy felt reduced to beggars. The beggars felt desperate. With nothing to lose, they picked up stones from the streets and looked for targets. Ruin was followed by riot and revolution: uprisings against Spanish rule in the Netherlands and Portugal, a ruinous civil war in France, and the Thirty Years' War (1618–1648), which involved most of Europe.

American silver was not the only cause of the upheavals in Europe, but threads of silver did link the various troubles. Still, as devastating as it was, the uproar in Europe was only "a kind of sideshow," in the words of two historians of the silver trade. Most of the American silver went to Asia. A large share of it ended up in the Chinese province of Fujian, in the port of Yuegang, with its history of both trade and piracy.

Fujian was the Chinese end of the galleon trade, in which Spanish ships sailed back and forth across the Pacific, carrying silver from Mexico and returning with goods from China. The actual trading took place in the Philippines, where the Spanish colonizers had first encountered Chinese traders in 1571. By the mid-1580s, Yuegang was sending twenty or more big junks to the Philippines every spring. As many as five hundred merchants crammed into each ship with every imaginable commodity to sell. Silk and porcelain were big parts of the trade, but the merchants also brought cotton, sugar, chestnuts, ivory, gems, furniture, cattle and horses, oranges, flour, and sugar—whatever they thought Europeans might want. The voyage was dangerous. Pirates routinely ambushed the junks.

When the junks arrived in the Philippines, the merchants docked across the bay from Manila. In the Parián the merchants met local Chinese sales agents, who knew how much silver the most recent galleons had brought, and who helped the sellers set their prices. It was a Chinese ghetto that the Spaniards had established outside Manila's walls. The Parián consisted of large warehouses surrounded by a maze of shopping areas crammed with stores, teahouses, and restaurants. The narrow streets were jammed at all hours with men in long, floppy-sleeved robes, embroidered silk shoes, and high round caps.

By 1591, twenty years after Legazpi entered Manila, the Parián had several thousand inhabitants. It dwarfed the official city of Manila, which had only a few hundred European colonists. For the Chinese, the arrangement was convenient. They had created a Chinese city outside China, far from the watchful eyes of Ming officials. For the Spaniards, the ghetto was alarming, alien, and unwelcome. It was also necessary. The Chinese would pay twice as much for Spanish silver as the rest of the world, and Chinese merchants were willing to sell silk and porcelain amazingly cheaply.

The Spanish court was dismayed by the size of the galleon trade. Too much silver was going out, and too many silks and porcelains were coming in. Somewhere between a third and half of the silver mined in the Americas went to China. Some of it went directly, through the galleon trade. Some went indirectly, when Europeans bought Chinese goods that had been carried overland from Asia by traders or shipped around Africa by the Dutch and Portuguese.

Either way, the result was that a lot of silver ended up in China. The Spanish monarchy was furious because the king wanted that silver to buy supplies and pay troops in Spain's many wars.

To cut back the galleon trade, officials announced that only two galleons would be allowed to cross the Pacific each year. The result was that merchants built bigger ships. The new galleons were enormous castles of the sea that could carry more than fifty tons of silver.

Much or most of that silver was illegal, meaning that it had not been officially registered for export. Worried Mexican officials informed the monarchy in 1602 that the galleons that year had exported almost four hundred tons of silver, eight times the amount that had been declared. In 1654 a galleon named the *San Francisco Javier* sank near Manila Bay. Official records claimed that it carried 418,323 pesos. Centuries later, divers found 1,180,865 aboard.

Authorities were unable to stop the smuggling of Mexican silver to China. It was too profitable. In an attempt to limit the trade at the other end, Spanish officials set a cap on the amount of silk and porcelain that could be bought at Manila.

Anything above that quota was supposed to be sent back to China. That didn't work, either. The Chinese and their sales agents simply unloaded the excess merchandise into waiting boats before they entered Manila Bay. The goods were then smuggled into the marketplace.

Spain had its own cloth-producing industry, and so did its colony in Mexico. Yet the Chinese silk industry was so large that Europeans couldn't compete. The Ming dynasty forced farmers to plant mulberry trees, which produce leaves that are the food for the silkworms from whose cocoons silk is made. Working in a frenzy, farmers up the river from Yuegang harvested silk five times a year. Other Chinese villages became hives of silk factories. Even though the Chinese merchants who sold the silk made huge profits, the Spanish merchants who bought it could resell it in the Americas for less than the cost of cloth made in Spain and still make their own profits. Amazingly, silk from China sold in Spain (after crossing both the Pacific and Atlantic oceans) for less than silk made in Spain.

Alarmed Europeans saw their textile mills threatened. European governments passed laws and regulations to limit the amount of Chinese

silk or clothing that could be imported, but the Chinese merchants found a way around every barrier, often with the help of the Spaniards in Manila. When the Spanish monarchy declared that silk could be imported only in chests of a certain size, the silk merchants designed special presses to mash huge quantities of cloth into each chest. The chests were packed so tightly that it took six men to carry one.

(left)
The source of silk:
silkworm cocoons.

"A FINE BOATLOAD OF WOODEN NOSES"

SPANISH COLONISTS IN MANILA FLOCKED TO THE Chinese ghetto in the Parián, outside the city walls, to buy items made by the craftspeople there. Chinese-made goods available in the shops of the Parián included everything from roof tiles to clothing in the latest European styles to marble statues of the Baby Jesus. These goods were "much prettier articles than are made in Spain, and sometimes so cheap that I am ashamed to mention it," wrote the bishop of the Philippines. European merchants griped about the competition. The monarchy ordered the shops moved farther away, but the Spaniards kept coming to them, attracted by the low prices.

The bishop noted that the trades once followed by the Spaniards had died out because people

were now buying their clothes and shoes from the Parián. As a warning, he told the story of what happened to one Spanish bookbinder, a man who practiced the trade of binding pages in leather covers to create books. He took a Chinese apprentice to help him with his work. After carefully watching the master bookbinder, the apprentice set up his own shop in the Parián and drove his master out of business. "His work is so good," wrote the bishop, "there is no need of the Spanish tradesman."

Not every Chinese business was successful. One shopkeeper sold a wooden nose to a Spanish man who had lost his nose in a duel. This inspired the shopkeeper to import "a fine boatload of wooden noses." Oddly enough, sales were poor.

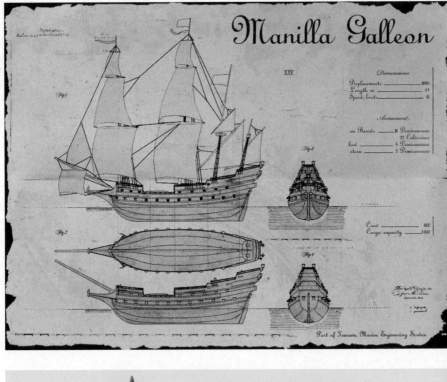

Manilla Galleon

XXV.

Dimensions.

Displacement _____ 1880
Length, m _____ 51
Speed, knots _____ 8

Armament.

on Boards _____ 8 Demicannons
                  22 Culverines
bond _____ 4 Demicannons
stern _____ 2 Demicannons

Crew _____ 800
Cargo capacity _____ 1000

Port of Tancale, Marine Engineering Service

A Magic Mountain and a Massacre

Business and politics constantly collided in the Spanish Philippines. On the business side, both the Spaniards in Manila and the Chinese in the Parián profited from the galleon trade and wanted it to continue. On the political side, however, the trade did not line up with the goals of the Spanish monarchy, which wanted to seize Asian lands, convert Asians to Christianity, and prevent the Dutch and Portuguese from expanding their power in Asia. The monarchy also wanted to limit the galleon trade and have as much silver as possible come to Spain instead of China, so it could pay for wars in Europe.

As a trading post, Manila benefited from having as few Spaniards as possible. It was expensive to send them there, and they kept dying of disease. Better to let the Chinese do all the work. Yet in political terms, Manila was an outpost of the Spanish empire. It made political sense for all important civic functions to remain in Spanish hands, and for the number and influence of the Chinese to be kept as low as possible. Every step in favor of commerce was against Spain's political interests, and every step in support of its political interests was against

(top left)
These enormous vessels were intended to carry huge loads of porcelain, silk, spices, and slaves across the Pacific. The journey across the great ocean was so rough that the ships were usually rebuilt after every passage.

(bottom left)
Frightened by the crowded Chinese ghetto called the Parián, Manila's few hundred resident Spaniards walled themselves off from it. To enter Manila, Parián residents walked across a moat and through a heavily guarded gate.

commerce. The tension is clear in the bloody saga of the magic mountain of Cavite.

The 1590s had seen several violent clashes between the Spaniards and the Chinese in Manila. A Spanish governor had forced hundreds of Chinese to serve as galley slaves, rowing ships with which he planned to conquer another island group. He mistreated them, and they mutinied, killing the governor and his crew. After that, the colony's leaders saw the Chinese as untrustworthy and dangerous. In 1596 the Manila government deported twelve thousand Chinese, forcing them out of the colony. In a few years they were as numerous as before, and the government was planning more deportations. Into this festering situation sailed three high Chinese officials in 1603. The three had been sent by the emperor of China to deliver a letter to the governor of Manila. According to the letter, rumors in China told of a magic mountain in Cavite, a long, skinny finger of land five miles from Manila, on the south side of the great bay. This mountain, said the letter, was full of gold and silver, all free for the taking. The three visitors had been sent to find out if it actually existed.

The expedition seems to have originated in some kind of daffy con job that bubbled through the Chinese court—not the only time such a thing happened during the Ming dynasty. Yet to the Spanish officials in Manila, who watched the three Chinese mandarins comb the colony for gold and silver, the expedition looked like a scouting party for an invasion. Surely these people could not be the pack of bumblers they appeared to be! They must be part of a sinister plot. While the governor debated whether to kill the three visitors, the visitors apologized for the mix-up and suddenly left.

Fearing that their departure was the signal for an invasion, the governor ordered his forces to destroy Chinese houses that were too close to Manila's defensive wall, to register every Chinese person in the Parián, and to get hold of every Chinese weapon. What happened next is hard to sort out, because the Spanish and Chinese accounts of events are wildly different.

In the Spanish version, angry Chinese mobs attacked a small band of the governor's soldiers, fled to the hills, and treacherously killed a representative of the governor who had come to negotiate for peace. To protect the Spanish citizens, the government sent troops into the hills. The Chinese rioters resisted, but they had few weapons and suffered heavy losses.

In the Chinese version of the story, there was no mob and no attack on soldiers. Instead, the government began a systematic massacre, killing the unarmed inhabitants of the Parián. Thousands of Chinese fled to the hills. They did kill the peace emissary, fearing his arrival was a trick, but when they went back to Manila for food, they were ambushed by the Spaniards. In the battle that followed, three hundred Spaniards and more than twenty-five thousand Chinese lost their lives.

Incredibly, just months later, the city leaders in Manila welcomed new Chinese immigrants. Spanish merchants were begging the trade junks to return because they wanted to buy cheap Chinese silk. Within two years the galleon trade and the Parián were almost back to normal. Yet the Spaniards in Manila were as few in numbers, as dependent on the Chinese, and as scared as before. Eventually they again tightened the limits on the Chinese. Rebellions flowered in the Parián, followed by deportations and massacres. The cycle repeated itself in 1639,

1662, 1686, 1709, 1755, 1763, and 1820, each time with an awful death toll.

Why would the Chinese keep returning? As much as the Spaniards craved silk, the Chinese craved silver. Yet the Ming court, like the Spanish monarchy, struggled with the conflict between trade as commerce and trade as a political tool of the state.

On one hand, silver from the silk trade became a source of imperial wealth and power. It paid for huge military projects, including much of the rebuilding of the Great Wall of China. It fueled an economic boom within China. On the other hand, the money that allowed business to grow also set off inflation, which had its worst impact on the poor. Also silver was a political threat because the dynasty did not control the source of the silver or the silver trade. The emperors could not limit the flow of silver into Fujian province, even if they wanted to, because of rampant smuggling. In the eyes of the court, the Fujianese merchants were people of doubtful loyalty who had created the Parián, a Chinese city that was outside imperial supervision. They were becoming wealthy and powerful in a way that was hard for the court to control.

The Chinese court does not seem to have foreseen the worst effect of the silver trade, however. As in Europe, so much silver flooded into China that its value eventually dropped. By about 1640, silver was worth no more in China than it was in the rest of the world. Unfortunately, the Ming dynasty required citizens to pay their taxes in a given weight of silver, not a given value. When the value dropped, people paid the same amount of silver they had always paid, but it was worth less. The Ming dynasty was suddenly short of money and couldn't pay for national defense. It was a bad time for the military to run out of money— China was under assault by northern groups now known as the Manchus. Over the course of decades, the Manchus gained control of China and became the Qing dynasty.

Dependence on foreign silver was not the only reason for the fall of the Ming dynasty, but the galleon trade played a part. Also, although the trade had brought China into the worldwide economic network of trade and commerce, the ecological part of the Columbian Exchange would have an equally large, equally unexpected effect on China.

(right)
The life stages of a silkworm, the small living engine of the Chinese silk industry.

Phalœna Mori or Silkworm

CHAPTER 6

LOVESICK GRASS, FOREIGN TUBERS, AND JADE RICE

TRADE BROUGHT MORE THAN SILVER ACROSS the Pacific. It also brought American plants to China, plants that would quickly change Chinese life.

Tobacco may have led the parade. It was as much a sensation in China as in England and Spain. One Chinese name for tobacco was "lovesick grass," for the way users became addicted to it. Ming soldiers embraced tobacco and spread the practice of smoking it as they marched around the empire. The fashionable rich showed off their tobacco addictions. Men boasted of being unable to eat, talk, or even think without a lighted pipe. Women carried special silk tobacco purses with jeweled fastenings. China's legions of enthusiastic smokers were

(left)
Four centuries after its introduction, tobacco remains so profitable in China that villagers still turn rice paddies into tobacco plots. These Fujianese farmers are drying tobacco in 2009.

not aware of tobacco's toxic effect on human health—that fact about tobacco was not clearly established until the twentieth century. By that time, China had been shaped, for better and worse, by tobacco and the other plants that came to China as part of the Columbian Exchange.

An Unplanned Ecological Invasion

Tobacco was only part of an unplanned ecological invasion that had far-reaching consequences. Tobacco sparked a smoking craze, but the other invaders changed China's food supply.

At the time that the Columbian Exchange began, China had about a quarter of the world's population. It had to feed these people on about a twelfth of the world's farmable land. At least half of the national diet consisted of rice and wheat. Unluckily, the areas within China that have enough water to grow rice and wheat are rather small.

China has many deserts, few big lakes, and irregular rainfall. It has only two big rivers, the Yangzi and the Huang He (Yellow River). Both run long, looping courses from the western mountains to the Pacific coast, emptying into the sea scarcely one hundred fifty miles from each other. The Yangzi carries water from the mountains to the rice-growing flatlands near the end of its course. The Huang He carries water into the North China Plain, the center of wheat production. Both areas are vital to feeding the nation, and both are prone to catastrophic floods. The Chinese imperial dynasties managed huge, complex systems of dams and canals to control the rivers and irrigate fields.

With little good farmland relative to the size of its population, China saw the Columbian Exchange, which brought new food plants, as a gift—and raced to embrace it. Sweet potatoes, corn, peanuts, chile peppers, pineapples, cashew nuts, and manioc (also called cassava) poured into Fujian province through the galleon trade, which had brought these plants from the Americas to the Philippines. The same plants reached other provinces by way of Dutch and Portuguese traders. All became part of Chinese life, and have remained so. Today China grows three-quarters of the world's sweet potatoes and is the second-largest producer of corn after the United States.

Sweet potatoes were probably native to Central America. Spanish ships carried them to the Philippines, where they were quickly adopted by the local people, who already grew the food plant taro, which has a big, starchy, sweet-tasting root. Like taro, the sweet potato has leaves and stems above the ground, while the edible part of the plant is a modified stem that stores nutrients below the surface. A Fujianese merchant had tasted sweet potatoes in the Philippines and liked them, so in the early 1590s he smuggled a few of the plants home past the Spanish cargo inspectors. (The inspectors did not mean to prevent the export of sweet potatoes specifically. They simply did not want to give away anything that might be profitable.)

Fujian was lucky that the sweet potato arrived when it did. The 1580s and 1590s were an intense part of the Little Ice Age in China. For two decades, hard floods had washed away the rice paddies of Fujian. Poor families were reduced to eating bark, grass, and insects. The son of the merchant who had brought the sweet potato to Fujian showed the tuber to the governor of Fujian, and soon the governor was instructing farmers to grow the new food crop.

Before long, four-fifths of the people in the port city of Yuegang were living on sweet potatoes. The crop spread through the province just in time for the fall of Beijing to the Manchus in 1644, which ushered in decades of violent chaos.

A group claiming to be a continuation of the Ming dynasty took root in Fujian after 1644. At the same time, pieces of the Ming military splintered away and became *wokou*, or pirates— while the actual *wokou* also took advantage of the confusion to step up their activities. To cut off food supplies to all these groups, the new Manchu dynasty, the Qing, forced the population in a 2,500-mile stretch of China's coastline to move into the interior of the country. Soldiers burned seaside villages and privately owned ships. Families had to leave with nothing but their clothing. Anyone who stayed behind was killed. For three decades the shoreline was empty of people for as far as fifty miles inland.

The coastal people flooded westward into the mountains of Fujian, Guangdong, and Zhejiang provinces. These highland areas were already inhabited, mostly by people from a different ethnic group, the Hakka. For a century poor Hakka and other mountain peoples had been migrating west into the mountains, renting highland areas that were too steep and too dry for rice farming. They cut and burned the tree cover and grew crops such as indigo (a plant that produces a blue dye) to sell. After a few years of slash-and-burn farming, the thin mountain soil was exhausted, and the Hakka moved on. Landless and poor, they were mocked as *pengmin*, or "shack people."

Because the shack people could not grow China's traditional wheat and rice on their steep rented fields, to feed themselves they turned to the new American crops. Corn can thrive in amazingly poor soil, and it grows quickly. Brought in from Portuguese traders, it became known in China as "jade rice." Sweet potatoes will grow where even corn cannot, tolerating soil with few nutrients. Another American import, the potato, originally bred in the Andes Mountains, also took root in the mountains of China. Yet in the decades after the American crops swept into China's highlands, the richest society in the world was thrown into turmoil by a struggle with its own environment—a struggle it lost.

A TRUE PIRATE KING

WHEN THE QING DYNASTY FORCED THE
people of coastal China inland in the middle of
the seventeenth century, the evacuation brought
an end to trade between the merchants of the
coast and the Spaniards in Manila. The only ones
able to carry on the trade were the *wokou*, or
pirates.

The pirate trade came under the control of a
man named Zheng Chenggong, who had spent
his life breaking the laws of the Ming dynasty.
When the Qing took over, Zheng realized that
the *wokou* had been better off under the Ming.
He led an enormous sea-based assault on
the Qing that came close to toppling the new

A seventeenth-
century portrait of
the powerful Ming-
dynasty pirate king,
Zheng Chenggong.

dynasty. Afterward he returned to piracy, with a fleet that one observer estimated at fifteen to twenty thousand vessels. Based in a palace across the river from the trade city of Yuegang, Zheng controlled China's entire southeast coast. He was a true pirate king.

Starting in 1657, Zheng carried on trade with Manila, exchanging Chinese goods for silver. Perhaps he was distracted by his ongoing battle with the Qing, because it took him until 1662 to realize two things. First, the Spaniards had no other source but him for silk and porcelain. Second, he, Zheng, was a pirate king with a huge fleet and a large army. He suggested a new trade arrangement to Manila. The Spaniards would give him all their silver, as before. In return, he would not kill them. Panicked, the Spaniards forcibly rounded up the Chinese in the Philippines, slaughtering many and sending the rest away on packed ships. This precaution turned out to be unnecessary. Two months later, Zheng died unexpectedly, probably of malaria. His sons fought over their inheritance, and the Manila trade was left alone.

The Qing had ordered the removal of people from the Chinese coast, but this had disastrous effects on them. Closing off the silver trade froze China's money supply. Because silver was always being wasted, lost, or hoarded and secretly buried, the pool of Chinese money was actually shrinking. The Qing reluctantly lifted the ban on the silver trade in 1681.

Catastrophe in the Highlands

In addition to forcing coastal people to move to the highlands of the interior, the Qing dynasty encouraged an even larger wave of migration into the dry, mountainous west. The Qing believed that sending people from the center of the country to occupy the thinly settled western hills, home to many non-Chinese peoples, was essential to the nation's destiny. Lured by tax benefits and cheap land, migrants from the east swarmed west. Most of the newcomers were as poor as the shack people. Like the shack people, they cut down trees and planted sweet potatoes, corn, and later potatoes on the steep slopes of their new homes. The amount of cropland in China soared. So did the amount of food grown—and the population. In some places the number of inhabitants grew by a hundred times in little more than a century.

For almost two thousand years, China's population had risen very slowly. This changed during and after the violent Qing takeover. Between the arrival of American crops and the end of the eighteenth century, China's population skyrocketed, possibly doubling to about 350 million people. Were the new crops

Qing-era China

- North China Plain
- Loess Plateau
- Desert

KOREA
JAPAN
Beijing
Huang He (Yellow River)
Shaanxi
Shandong
Jiangsu
Shanghai
Sichuan
Hubei
Yangzi River
Zhejiang
Jiangxi
Tibet
Guizhou
Fujian
Yuegang
Yunnan
Guangxi
Guangdong
TAIWAN
Guangzhou
Pacific Ocean
LUZON

China Floods
1823

Flooded areas
- Prolonged, severe (1's)
- Shorter duration (2's)

Beijing
Huang He (Yellow River)
Dazhai
Nanjing
Wuhan
Anqing
Yangzi River
Yuegang
Guangzhou
Pacific Ocean

the only reason for this population boom?

No. The crops arrived as the Qing were already transforming China. The ambitious dynasty fought disease and hunger in many ways. The Qing started the world's first program of inoculations to protect people from smallpox. They enlarged the nationwide network of food storehouses that bought grain and sold it at low, state-controlled prices during shortages. Still, most of the population increase took place in areas with American crops. The families that the Qing encouraged to move west needed to eat, and what they ate, day in and day out, was sweet potatoes, corn, and later potatoes. Part of the reason China is the world's most populous nation is the Columbian Exchange.

The huge increase in cropland came with consequences. Once trees were cut from steep slopes, rainwater rushed downhill, carrying soil nutrients with it. Farmers unfamiliar with raising corn did not at first realize that planting rows straight up and down the hills, rather than in lines across the slope, would channel the rain down the slope, worsening soil erosion. Also, people who merely rented their fields, unlike owners, were not strongly motivated to fertilize

(left)
Corn at the edge of the Gobi Desert, in Inner Mongolia.

the soil with ashes and manure to replace the nutrients that went into their crops or were washed away by flowing water. As a result, soil in the newly farmed hills quickly deteriorated.

Deforestation in the hills also caused disaster below, in the flatlands along the rivers. Rainfall went down the hills in sheets, instead of being absorbed by trees. The rivers swelled and poured over their banks in devastating floods. Drowned rice paddies of the lower Yangzi drove up the price of rice, which encouraged more corn production in the highlands, which drowned more rice in the valleys. Floods became more frequent as more shack people moved into the mountains. Worse, the floods mostly targeted China's major agricultural centers, the rich farmlands along the lower Yangzi and Huang He (Yellow) Rivers.

Part of the problem was large-scale immigration, but part of it was a legal loophole. The income from farms was taxed, but the income from rental property was not. Landowners who had property in the highlands had an easy source of untaxable income by renting that property out to shack people and migrants. The deforestation of their highland property might contribute to floods that would affect their own fields in the lowlands, but the risk of floods was spread across a whole region, while the income from their rental property was theirs alone. Local business interests with rental property beat down every attempt to rein in the shack people. It was an environmentalist's nightmare. The shortsighted pursuit of small-scale profits steered a course for long-range, large-scale disaster.

Constant floods led to constant famine and constant unrest. Repairing the damage of the floods drained the resources of the state. American silver may have pushed the Ming dynasty over the edge. American crops certainly helped kick out the underpinnings of the tottering Qing dynasty, which collapsed in 1911. To be sure, other things contributed to the fall of the Qing. A rebellion led by a Hakka mystic tore apart the state, and a series of weak emperors did nothing to combat government corruption. The empire also lost two wars with Great Britain, which forced China to open its borders to the British-backed trade in the narcotic drug opium. Yet the path to the Qing downfall had been opened by the Columbian Exchange.

Unlearning from Dazhai

In 1963, floods ravaged Dazhai, a village of a few hundred people in the dry, knotted hills of north-central China. Standing in the wreckage, the local secretary of the Communist Party refused aid from the state and promised that Dazhai would rebuild itself—and create a new, more productive village. He was as good as his word. Harvests soon soared, in spite of the flood and the infertile soil.

Mao Zedong was the head of the Communist state that had taken control of China in the mid-twentieth century. He was delighted by Dazhai's increase in food production. Mao bused thousands of local officials to Dazhai, telling them to copy what they saw there. Mainly, they saw peasants working furiously to build terraces from the top to the bottom of each hill. They vowed to do the same in their villages. Filled with excitement, and lashed on by their local officials, villagers fanned out across the hills, cutting the scrubby trees, slicing the slopes into terraces, and planting what they could on every surface. The terraces turned unplantable steep slopes into new farmland.

Dazhai is located in a geological formation

called the Loess Plateau, an area about the size of France, Belgium, and the Netherlands combined. For ages, winds have swept across the deserts to the west, blowing grit and sand into the Loess Plateau. This has created vast heaps of packed silt—or loess, as geologists call it. Loess doesn't form soil so much as pack together like wet snow—when it is dry. Yet silt piles are easy to wash away. They don't clump together firmly. If silt grains are knocked free by flowing water, they move easily. Washed down steep hills, these particles can be carried great distances. The Huang He makes a big loop right through the Loess Plateau. It carries an enormous burden of silt from the plateau right into the North China Plain, the country's agricultural heartland.

Because the plain is flat, the water slows down and deposits silt on the bottom and along the banks. The silt renews the soil, which is one reason the plain is so good for agriculture. At the same time, though, the silt builds up the riverbed and banks, raising the Huang He one to three inches above the surrounding countryside each year. Over time, the river has lifted itself as much as forty feet above the land around it. Every so often the Huang He overflows or breaks its banks, creating a ruinous flood. In the eighteenth and nineteenth centuries, erosion on the Loess Plateau caused more frequent, and more lethal, floods in the plain. Chinese court records show that excess silt made the Huang He overflow its banks in huge floods a dozen times between 1780 and 1850. A flood in 1887 was among the deadliest ever recorded, with the number of deaths estimated at up to a million.

The cause of the flooding (deforestation of the Loess Plateau to plant corn and sweet potatoes) was well known. Yet the government did nothing about it, and neither did the landlords who rented to the shack people. Instead, the floods continued until the Qing dynasty fell, an event that the floods had helped bring about— which made it all the more incredible when Mao Zedong ordered more land cleared in the Loess Plateau, in the Dazhai style. In the 1960s and 1970s the steepest hillsides were targeted to be turned into productive farmland. Yet the terrace walls, made of nothing but packed earth, constantly fell apart. During the "Dazhai era," as this period was called, soil erosion into the Huang He increased by about a third.

The consequences were dire and easy to see.

As nutrients washed out of the soil, harvests fell, forcing huge numbers of farmers to become migrants. The Loess Plateau, which once caught dust from the desert, began producing dust clouds of its own as its dry, exposed soil blew away. Vaclav Smil, a geographer who has made a long study of China's environment, says, "It must be one of the greatest wastes of human labor in history. Tens of millions of people being forced to work night and day, most of it on projects that a child could have seen were a terrible stupidity. Cutting down trees and planting grain on steep slopes—how could that be a good idea?"

In an effort to halt deforestation, the government in 1981 required every able-bodied citizen older than eleven to plant three to five trees a year whenever possible. Three years earlier Beijing had launched what may be the world's biggest ecological project: planting a 2,800-mile-long band of trees across northeast, north, and northwest China. Scheduled to be completed in 2050, this Green Wall of China is supposed to slow down the winds that drive desertification and dust storms.

To remedy the damage to soil in places such

Beginning in the 1960s, farmers in China's Loess Plateau stripped the forest and carved terraces out of the hills. Because the loess erodes easily, every rainfall caused damage to the terraces. Eventually, the terraces built on the steepest slopes collapsed. Farmers tried to make a living on hills almost too steep to stand on.

as Dazhai, farmers are now following the "3-3-3" system. They replant a third of their land (the steepest, most erosion-prone slopes) with grass and trees, which are natural barriers to erosion. They plant orchards of food-producing trees on another third. On the final, flattest third, they plant crops that they fertilize. Local officials are rewarded for the number of trees they plant, but unfortunately they have not been required to choose tree species that are suited to local conditions. Also, while the government has the power to order whole villages into the hills to plant millions of trees, farmers have little reason to water or care for trees they cannot use just because the trees supposedly stop erosion miles from their homes.

The result is fields of dead trees. When I visited Shaanxi province in the Loess Plateau, farmers told me, "Every year we plant trees, but no trees survive." During my visit, lines of dead trees dotted the slopes, stretching for miles. The harvest was over, and farmers were about to be marched back for another round of planting. Despite previous failures, China's government is trying, tree by tree, to undo the accidental legacy of the global silver trade.

(right)
Sweet potatoes in China are often eaten raw, the skin whittled until they look somewhat like ice-cream cones.

A crop of potatoes with flowers in full bloom.

PART FOUR

EUROPE IN THE WORLD

HOW AND WHY DID EUROPE AND THE EUROPEAN
colonies that became the United States emerge
as a controlling power in the world? Much of the
answer lies in two revolutions, each involving
a South American plant that was introduced to
other parts of the world through the Columbian
Exchange.

The potato originated in Peru and Bolivia. It
fueled the Agricultural Revolution, which began
in late-seventeenth-century Europe and changed
the way people around the world produced food.
The rubber tree originated in Brazil. It was an
essential part of the Industrial Revolution, which
took off in the early and mid-nineteenth century
and changed energy use, manufacturing,
warfare, and a host of other human activities
everywhere on earth. Both revolutions, the
agricultural and the industrial, supported
the rise of the West. Both would have been
dramatically different without the Columbian
Exchange.

CHAPTER 7

POTATO POWER, POTATO PESTS

WHEN POTATO PLANTS BLOOM, THEY SEND UP
flowers that bob in the fields like fat purple stars.
Tradition says that Marie Antoinette, the queen
of France who met her death by guillotine in
1793, liked them so much that she put them
in her hair in happier, pre-guillotine days. Her
husband, King Louis XVI, supposedly put one of
the blossoms in his buttonhole, inspiring a brief
fad in which French aristocrats swanned around
with potato flowers in their clothes.

The potato, which is not related to the
sweet potato, came originally from the Andes
Mountains of South America. Today it is the
fifth most important crop in the world, after
sugarcane, wheat, corn, and rice. Compared
to grain, a tuber such as the potato is more

productive. If the edible head of a grain or rice plant grows too large or heavy, the plant will fall over, with fatal results. Tubers grow underground and do not face this weight limitation. In 2008 a farmer in Lebanon dug up a potato that weighed almost twenty-five pounds. In photographs it was bigger than his head.

Many scholars believe that the introduction of the potato to Europe was a key moment in history. At the time the potato was adopted as a staple food, famine ended in northern Europe. (The same thing happened with corn, on a smaller scale, in southern Europe.) In the view of historian William H. McNeill, the potato led to empire. He argued that potatoes, by feeding fast-growing populations, allowed a handful of European nations to dominate most of the world between 1750 and 1950. The end of hunger in European nations created political stability, which let those nations take advantage of the flood of silver from the Americas. The potato fed the rise of the West.

The potato had an equally important effect on agriculture. By adopting the potato, Europe and North America set a pattern for modern large-scale agriculture, sometimes called the farm-

(*left*)
Children working in the potato fields near East Grand Forks, Minnesota, 1937.

industry or agro-industrial complex. This type of agriculture rests on three pillars: improved crops, high-intensity fertilizers, and factory-made pesticides, which are chemicals that kill bothersome insects and microorganisms. These three were deliberately brought together in the 1950s and 1960s to create the Green Revolution, an explosion in agricultural productivity that changed farms from Illinois to Indonesia. It also set off a political argument about the world's food supply that grows more intense by the day. All three pillars of the farm-industry complex—crops, fertilizers, and pesticides—rose from the Columbian Exchange.

The Food of the Inka

In terms of geography, the Andes were an unlikely place for the creation of a major staple food. The chain of Andes peaks is the second-biggest mountain range on the planet, after the Himalayas. It forms a fifty-five-hundred-mile barrier, sometimes twenty-two thousand feet high, along the Pacific coast of South America. The main part of the range is three parallel mountain chains separated by high plains called the altiplano. The altiplano has a wet season and a dry season, with most of the rain coming between November and March. Left on its own, it would be covered by grasses.

From this unpromising landscape sprang one of the world's great cultural traditions. While Egyptians were building the pyramids thousands of years ago, Andean societies built their own monumental temples and ceremonial plazas. There were many highly developed Andean societies, but the most famous today are the Inka, who seized most of the Andes in a few violent decades, built great highways and cities splendid with gold, and then fell to Spanish disease and Spanish soldiers in the sixteenth century.

Potatoes were eaten in the region long before the Andean societies arose. Archaeologists have found evidence of people eating potatoes in southern Chile thirteen thousand years ago. Their food was not the modern domestic potato, which is the species *Solanum tuberosum*. Instead they ate a wild relative of the domestic potato that still grows on the coast. Scientists are not sure exactly how Andean cultures eventually created the domestic potato, only that they were eating completely domesticated potatoes by 2000 BC, if not earlier.

Andean natives ate potatoes boiled, baked, and mashed as people in Europe and North America do today. They also ate potatoes in many other forms, including chuño, which is made by spreading potatoes outside to freeze on cold nights, letting them thaw in the morning sun, then leaving them to freeze again the next night. The water inside the potato cells freezes, rupturing the cell walls. Repeated freeze-thaw cycles turn the spuds into soft, mushy blobs. Farmers squeeze out the water, and what remains is chuño, stiff chunks about two-thirds smaller and lighter than the original tubers. Cooked into a spicy Andean stew, chuño resembles gnocchi, the potato-flour dumplings of central Italy. Chuño can be kept for years without refrigeration, meaning that it can be stored as a food supply in case of bad harvests. This was the food of the conquering Inkan armies.

Farming the Andes was and is a struggle against geography. The terrain is steep. Wind and water easily erode the soil. To manage water and control erosion, Andean people built more than a million acres of agricultural terraces. A Spanish voyager marveled in 1572 that the terraces were carved into the hillsides like stair

(right)
Using a foot plow, Andean Indians break up the ground in this drawing from about 1615. Women follow behind to sow seed potatoes.

212

tienpo de la bransa— hayllinmi ynca—

hacra

steps. (The soils in the Andes are not made of loess, and the terraces were often faced with stone, so they did not promote erosion as in the case of the Dazhai-style terraces in China.)

Andean people also farmed on flatter land in the valleys, planting their crops in raised beds or ridges of dug-up earth. They used every scrap of the potato plant except for the fruits, which are toxic. People ate the potatoes, used the dried stalks for cooking fuel, and fed the leaves to their llamas and alpacas. (The alpaca, like the llama, is a relative of the camel that is native to South America.)

People planted different varieties of potatoes depending on how far up or down the mountains their fields were located. Farmers also cultivated multiple kinds of potatoes to have a variety of tastes. Plant researchers have found fields in Andean villages where as many as twenty different varieties of potato are grown. The International Potato Center in Peru has preserved more than 3,700 of these traditional varieties, which are called landraces. Farmers there now also produce modern, Idaho-style potato breeds for the market, although they consider these potatoes bland and fit only for city people.

(right)
Andean natives bred hundreds of different potato varieties, most of them still never seen outside South America.

The Andean potato is less a single species than
an agglomeration of many related species, each
divided into multiple landraces. Even *S. tuberosum*,
the modern potato, has eight broad types. Wild
potatoes are as confusing as domestic ones, with
many varieties and hybrids. A study in 1990
identified 229 species of wild potato. None of
this great variety was understood by the Spanish
conquistadors, led by Francisco Pizarro, who
landed in Ecuador in 1532 and attacked the Inka.
The conquistadors simply noticed locals eating
round objects, and copied them.

From a Sea to a Teaspoon
Once the conquistadors started eating potatoes,
word of the new food spread rapidly beyond South
America. Within three decades, Spanish farmers
in the Canary Islands, off the northwest coast of
Africa, were growing enough potatoes to export
them to the Netherlands, which was then part of the
Spanish Empire. The first scientific description of
the potato appeared in 1596. Yet the potato was slow
to take root outside the Spanish colonies. When the
German state of Prussia was hit by famine in 1744,
King Frederick the Great, a supporter of spuds, had
to order the peasants to eat potatoes.

France was especially slow to adopt the new crop. So up stepped a trained pharmacist and potato booster named Antoine-Augustin Parmentier, the Johnny Appleseed of the potato. Parmentier had served in the army and was captured and held prisoner for three years by the Prussians. During that time he ate little but potatoes, a diet that, to his surprise, kept him in good health.

Parmentier became one of the first scientists to try to figure out what was in food and how it sustained the body. When crops failed in eastern France in 1769 and 1770, a local academy asked for essays on foods that could be substituted for "Regular Foods." Seven essays were submitted. Five of them promoted the potato, but Parmentier's essay was the most passionate and well documented. It launched his career as a potato activist.

A few years later, the king of France removed price controls on grain. Bread prices rose, sparking more than three hundred civil disturbances. Parmentier claimed that France would stop fighting over bread if the French just tried potatoes. He set up pro-spud publicity stunts, such as serving an all-potato dinner to high-society guests and planting forty acres of potatoes at the edge of Paris, knowing that the famished poor would steal them.

It was Parmentier who persuaded the king to wear potato blossoms in his buttonhole. His efforts were successful. Potato cultivation spread, and the potato became a staple in many European nations.

Parmentier had not just praised the potato. He had changed it, although he did not realize this. All of the potatoes in Europe descended from just a few tubers sent across the Atlantic by curious Spaniards. In terms of genetics, the European potato had been created by dipping a teaspoon into the sea of potato genes in Peru and Bolivia. Parmentier urged people to cultivate this limited sample on a massive scale. Because potatoes are grown from pieces of tuber, and each piece grows into a potato identical to its source, Parmentier was unknowingly promoting the idea of planting huge areas with clones. The result was what agricultural scientists call a monoculture, the cultivation of a single kind of plant. The potato fields Parmentier imagined spreading across Europe were drastically different from potato fields in the Andes. In the homeland of the potato, the fields were a colorful patchwork of many varieties. In Europe, they were an orderly array of identical plants.

A DUBIOUS TUBER

EUROPEANS REGARDED POTATOES WITH fascinated suspicion. The potato was the first food they had seen that was grown from tubers rather than seeds. Some people believed that potatoes aroused sexual desire. Others feared that they caused diseases such as leprosy. Russian priests declared that potatoes were evil. Their proof? The potato is not mentioned in the Bible. A pro-potato English alchemist, in contrast, claimed that potatoes cured tuberculosis. English farmers were more doubtful. Because the potato came from Spain's colonies in the Americas, and Spain was a Catholic nation, they regarded the potato as an advance scout for Roman Catholicism, which they hated.

A French writer named Denis Diderot took a

position in the middle in his *Encyclopedia*, which was published between 1751 and 1765. "No matter how you prepare it, the root is tasteless and starchy," he wrote. "It cannot be regarded as an enjoyable food, but it provides abundant, reasonably healthy food for men who want nothing but sustenance." Diderot viewed the potato as "windy," meaning that it caused gas. Still, he gave it a thumbs-up. "What," he asked, "is windiness to the strong bodies of peasants and laborers?"

Fighting Famine

The potato's effects on Europe were striking. Hunger was a familiar presence in Europe during the Little Ice Age, when cold weather killed crops even as Spanish silver drove up the price of food. When harvests failed, food riots followed. French historian Fernand Braudel reported that there were thousands of such riots across Europe between 1400 and 1700. Rioters, often led by women, broke into bakeries and grain storehouses and either stole food or forced merchants to accept a "just" price. Ravenous bandits swarmed the highways, seizing convoys that carried grain to cities. Authorities turned to violent action to restore order.

Just as sweet potatoes and corn had provided new foods to combat China's hunger crisis, the potato was the salvation of Europe's starving poor. Potatoes produced about four times as much food per acre as wheat. Along with corn, potatoes became in much of Europe what they already were in the Andes: an ever-dependable staple, something eaten at every meal.

In places such as France, potatoes became an essential supplement to wheat. In Ireland, potatoes almost replaced wheat. Roughly 40 percent of people in Ireland ate no solid food other than potatoes. The same was true of 10 to 30 percent of people in the Netherlands, Belgium, Prussia, and perhaps Poland. In potato country, a two-thousand-mile band that stretched from Ireland to the Ural Mountains of Russia, famine almost disappeared. The arrival of the potato meant that Europe, at long last, could grow its own dinner.

The potato did not just increase farm production; it made farm production more reliable. Potatoes could be harvested just three months after planting, or left in the ground for months to prevent their being seized by hungry soldiers on the march. The result was that Europe's food supply became more stable as well as larger—and the result of this improved food supply was population growth.

Just as the arrival of sweet potatoes and corn in China had contributed to a population boom, the number of people in Europe roughly doubled in the century after the potato was introduced. The Irish, who ate more potatoes than anyone else, had the biggest boom. Ireland's population grew from perhaps 1.5 million in the early 1600s to about 8.5 million, maybe more, two centuries later. The increase did not happen because potato eaters had more children. It happened because more of their children survived. Potatoes did more than just prevent deaths from famine. They produced better-nourished people who were less likely to die of infectious disease, the main killer of the time.

American crops were not the only reason for China's population boom, and the same was true in Europe. The potato arrived in the midst of other changes in food production. Better roads and transportation networks made it easier to ship food to places with poor harvests. Marshlands and high pastures were reclaimed for farming. People were learning to use manure from farm animals as fertilizer and were planting clover to restore nutrients to the soil. Also as in China, the chill of the Little Ice Age began to draw to an end. The potato, however, played a big part in Europe's long boom and the birth of the modern era.

The Gift of Guano

Thirteen miles off the coast of Peru is a group of dry, rocky mounds called the Chincha Islands. Large colonies of seabirds, especially

the Peruvian cormorant, Peruvian pelican, and Peruvian booby, have nested on the islands for thousands of years. Over time they covered the islands with a layer of guano (their excrement, or waste) that was as much as one hundred fifty feet thick.

Guano makes excellent fertilizer. Centuries ago the natives of the Andes discovered that guano could restore nutrients to soil that had lost them by being farmed repeatedly. Llama trains carried baskets of Chincha guano along the coast. The Inka managed the guano resource carefully. They parceled out guano claims to individual villages and fined people for disturbing the birds while they were nesting. When the Spaniards arrived, they were too blinded by the shine from Potosí silver to pay attention to the guano-hauling habits of the people they had conquered. The first European to observe guano carefully was Friedrich Wilhelm Heinrich Alexander von Humboldt of Germany, who traveled through South America between 1799 and 1804. Humboldt, a brilliant man, was a pioneer in botany, geography, astronomy, geology, and anthropology. He was insatiably curious about everything that crossed

(left and page 227) Thousands of Chinese slaves mined the guano of Peru's Chincha Islands, shown here in 1865, for export to Europe as fertilizer. The islands had a layer of guano as much as 150 feet deep.

his path, including the fleet of native guano boats he saw skittering along the coast of Peru.

"One can smell them a quarter of a mile away," he wrote. "The sailors, accustomed to the ammonia smell, aren't bothered by it; but we couldn't stop sneezing as they approached." Among the thousands of samples Humboldt took back to Europe was a bit of Peruvian guano, which he sent to two French chemists. They found that Chincha guano was 11 to 17 percent nitrogen, a substance that plants need and that soil often lacks, especially if it has been farmed over and over. A few bags of guano appeared in European ports in the 1830s. Then, in 1840, a highly respected chemist praised guano as a fertilizer in his new book. Farmers who read the book, many of them big landowners, raced to buy guano and spread it on their fields. Their crop yields doubled, even tripled!

Guano mania took hold. In 1841, Britain imported 1,880 tons of Peruvian guano. Four years later the figure had risen to 219,764 tons. In forty years, Peru exported 14 million tons of guano. It was the beginning of a key feature of modern agriculture: transferring huge amounts of crop nutrients from one place to another

using systems based on scientific research.

The Peruvian government took over the Chincha Islands but soon discovered that no one wanted to work there. On the barren, waterless, stinking islands, guano miners had to work, eat, and sleep on shelves of ancient bird excrement. The government sent convicts, army deserters, and African slaves to the islands, but the arrangement didn't work out. The convicts and deserters killed one another, and the slaves were so valuable that their owners on the mainland did not want to part with them.

In 1849, Peru gave up trying to run the mines and turned the guano operation over to Peru's biggest cotton grower, who was also one of its main slave owners. He was supposed to mine the guano with his own slaves, but he did not want to take them away from his cotton fields, so he recruited workers from China. The workers were told they would have to pay for their passage across the Pacific by working for eight years in the gold fields of California. Their real destination, the guano islands, was not mentioned.

The unfortunate Chinese who came to Peru, as many as one hundred thousand of them, were treated as slaves. They suffered brutal treatment and horrible conditions during their passage and on the islands. After journalists wrote about the guano slavery and caused an international scandal, the government of Peru turned the guano contract over to someone else. All the while guano flowed to Europe and North America, carried by a British shipping company. Americans fumed with resentment at the high prices both Peru and the British shippers charged them. In 1856 the U.S. Congress passed the Guano Islands Act, which gave American citizens the right to seize any guano islands they saw. By 1903 the U.S. Department of State had recognized claims to sixty-six islands or coral atolls. Most proved to have little guano and were quickly abandoned. Nine remain under U.S. control today.

Before the potato and corn, before intensive use of fertilizer, European living standards were roughly the same as those today in Bangladesh. On average, European peasants ate less each day than hunter-gatherer societies in Africa or the Amazon. Industrial monoculture, with improved crops and high-intensity fertilizer, allowed Europe and then the rest of the world to produce enough food to keep up with population growth. Living standards doubled or tripled worldwide even as the population climbed from fewer than a billion people in 1700 to more than seven billion today.

Guano set the pattern for modern agriculture, in which farmers dump bags of chemical nutrients into the land. The nutrients are shipped from far-off places or made in distant factories. Farming is the act of turning those nutrients into crops in the field: high volumes of nitrogen go in, high volumes of potatoes or corn come out. Along the way, guano was almost entirely replaced by nitrates, nitrogen compounds that were mined from vast deposits in the deserts of Chile, Peru's neighbor. The nitrates in turn were replaced by artificial fertilizers made in factories by a process invented in the early twentieth century. Yet, like all human activities, the rise of modern agriculture had its downside.

The guano trade that launched modern agriculture marked the beginning of one of the worst pitfalls of the Columbian Exchange: the carrying of pests from one part of the world to others. Proof might never be found, but experts believe that the guano ships carried a microscopic stowaway named *Phytophthora infestans*. This microorganism belongs to a group called the water molds and is a cousin to algae. It causes late blight, a plant disease that exploded through Europe's potato fields in the 1840s. Famine caused by the blight killed as many as two million people (half of them in Ireland) in what came to be known as the Great Hunger.

The Great Hunger
The name *Phytophthora infestans* means "vexing plant destroyer." The microorganism sends out spores that swim through moisture on the stems and leaves of plants. If the day is warm and wet enough, the spores infiltrate the leaf cells. Threadlike filaments lace through much of the plant, preparing new spores. *P. infestans* preys on members of the nightshade family, which includes potatoes, tomatoes, eggplants, and sweet peppers. Washed into the soil, it attacks roots and tubers as much as six inches below the surface. Once it strikes a potato, it turns the outer flesh into dry, grainy, red-brown rot. Blight reaches like dark claws toward the center of the tuber. The entire potato must usually be thrown away, but carefully, because a single infected

potato can produce a million *P. infestans* spores. Most likely the blight traveled from Peru to Europe aboard a guano ship. It probably came to Antwerp, in Belgium, where farmers were experimenting with new varieties of potatoes from the Americas, hoping to find types that would resist European plant diseases. The potatoes they imported almost certainly made their journey on a guano ship. Chances are high that one of those ships unknowingly carried potatoes infected with blight that infected a whole continent.

The new potatoes were planted in 1844. That summer a botanist observed a few plants with bruiselike spots, a sign of infected leaves— although Europeans did not yet know the symptoms of blight. By the next summer, blight had spread from its launching pad in Belgium to France, the Netherlands, Germany, Denmark, and England. Blight was first reported in Ireland in September 1845.

Ireland, one of the poorest nations in Europe, was also one of the most dependent on the potato. At a stroke, the blight removed the food supply from half the country. There was no money to buy grain from outside. The

(*left and following page*)
In 1847, an artist for the *Illustrated London News* toured the famine-wracked Irish countryside. His reports on a landscape of ruins and starving beggars brought the crisis to the attention of the English public.

result was horrific. Soon Ireland resembled a postapocalyptic landscape. Starving, impoverished men in rags lined the roads and slept in ditches. People ate dogs, rats, and tree bark. Reports of cannibalism were frequent. Entire families died in their homes and were eaten by pets gone feral. Diseases such as dysentery, smallpox, and measles picked away at the survivors.

Life became a struggle of all against all. Starving men crept into fields to steal turnips. Farmers dug mantraps in their fields to stop them. Neighbor fought neighbor for food and shelter. Crime levels exploded. Some people stole to put food on their tables. Others stole knowing that at least they would be fed in jail.

Hundreds of thousands of people fled Ireland in what became known as "coffin ships" because so many died aboard them. Most of the surviving migrants went to the United States or Canada. The famine broke Ireland. At a million or more deaths, it was one of history's deadliest famines, in terms of the percentage of the population lost. A similar famine in the United States today would kill almost forty million people. (The only worse famine may have occurred in 1918–1922 in the Soviet Union, a former state made up of Russia and neighboring republics.) Within a decade of the blight, another two million people fled Ireland, and many more followed. Even today Ireland has the sad distinction of being the only nation in Europe, perhaps in the world, to have fewer people within the same boundaries than it had one hundred fifty years ago.

What made Europe so vulnerable to *P. infestans*? For one thing, the potato crop was highly uniform. About half the potatoes in Ireland were clones of a single variety of a single species. Monoculture can be productive, but it can also be a drawback when plant diseases attack. In a mix of many different varieties, some varieties might prove more resistant to a given disease. When all plants are the same, if one falls, they all fall.

Another reason for Europe's vulnerability had to do with a change in farming methods. Farmers in Ireland and across northern Europe had traditionally grown crops by cutting out blocks of soil, flipping them over, piling them into long ridges separated by furrows, and

(top right)
Spread of Potato Blight, 1845

(bottom right)
A potato cut in half showing the classic red-brown rot caused by *P. infestans*.

planting their crops on the tops of these ridges. It was a method very much like the traditional raised beds of Andean farmers. This method, called lazy-bed farming, discouraged many plant diseases because it let wet soil dry out.

Eighteenth-century agricultural reformers promoted new methods, however. The reformers called lazy beds inefficient because the wide spaces between the rows weren't planted with crops. They wanted to cover every inch of the fields and use new, factory-made machines to plow the soil deeply and harvest every bit of the crop. These machines needed flat, level fields. After about 1750, as the new methods took hold, the lazy beds began to disappear. They were almost gone from Ireland by 1834. A modern researcher has discovered, however, that potatoes in lazy beds are less vulnerable to blight than those in level, plowed fields. Lazy beds also have fewer weeds and need less fertilizer than those in flat fields.

The blight that caused the Great Hunger was not the first plant disease to attack potatoes in Europe, but it was the worst. It took advantage of the new, scientific agriculture: one kind of potato, grown in level

(right)
Lazy-bed cultivation, as it was called in English, was common in Ireland until the early nineteenth century. The abandonment of lazy-beds likely helped potato blight race through the countryside, worsening the great famine.

fields that were shaped for technology rather than biology. Before many years had passed, potatoes in the United States would come under attack from a different pest, another hitchhiker on the Columbian Exchange.

"War upon the Beetles"

In 1861, beetles overran a potato garden in Kansas. The farmer had never seen a beetle like this: a third of an inch long, with a yellow-orange body and tigerish black stripes. There were so many of them that he could hardly see the leaves of his potato plant through the swarms of tiny, glittering bodies.

The same beetle invaded Iowa and Kansas that summer. It spread steadily north and east, advancing its range by fifty to a hundred miles each year. By 1870 it had reached Michigan. Seven years later it was attacking potatoes from Maine to North Carolina. Farmers had no idea where the beetle had come from, or how to stop it.

In Europe, the Great Hunger was still a vivid memory. Reports of potato devastation alarmed the continent. A number of countries banned the import of American potatoes, but Great

Britain did not. The beetle was carried to Europe in ships' holds and eventually established itself there. Today it occupies Europe from Athens, Greece, to Stockholm, Sweden. In the Americas its realm reaches from south-central Mexico to north-central Canada. Many biologists fear that it will spread to Asia and complete its round-the-world journey.

This pest is now known as the Colorado potato beetle, although it did not come from Colorado, and it was not at first interested in potatoes. The beetle originated in south-central Mexico. Its diet centered on a wild plant called buffalo bur, which is a relative of the potato.

Scientists think that the beetle was found only in Mexico until the Spanish conquistadors, agents of the Columbian Exchange, brought horses and cattle to the Americas. Quickly recognizing the usefulness of these animals, Indians stole as many as they could and sent them north for their families to ride and eat. Buffalo bur came along in the form of spiny seedpods tangled in the horses' manes, cows' tails, and native saddlebags. After reaching Texas, buffalo bur could also have been carried in the shaggy fur

of bison, or buffalo. The beetle followed in the path of the buffalo bur, its favorite food. By 1819 the beetle was seen feeding on buffalo bur along the Missouri River. There it met the potato, and a quirk of genetics brought insect and tuber together.

In Mexico, the beetles prefer buffalo bur to potatoes. If a beetle is placed on a potato leaf, it will go elsewhere in search of food. Yet one beetle in the American Midwest in the middle of the nineteenth century was born with a tiny, random mutation, maybe something as small as a speck of DNA that got flipped end to end. That mutation was not enough to make the beetle look different or keep it from reproducing, but it may have been enough to turn its focus from buffalo bur to potato. This single genetic accident, passed on to that beetle's descendants and then on and on to their millions and millions of descendants, was enough to create a worldwide problem. The Colorado potato beetle is the potato's most devastating pest to this day.

Insects have bothered farmers since people first began planting crops. Yet large-scale industrial agriculture changed the game. For

(left)
Many Andean peoples have long grown potatoes in parallel ridges, which discourages fungal diseases by letting the soil dry.

thousands of years the beetle had made do with the buffalo bur scattered through the Mexican hills, mingled among many other plant species. Compared to that, a potato farm—hundreds of orderly rows of a single type of a single species—was an ocean of breakfast. By adapting to feed on potatoes, the beetle gained access to more food than it had ever had before. Naturally, its population exploded. So did that of other pests, such as the potato blight, that took advantage of the same opportunities.

Each of the massive new farms was a storehouse of riches for the species that could exploit it—and because farms grew more and more alike, with growers planting just a few varieties of a single species, pests could jump from farm to farm. Even the jumping was easier than ever, thanks to the modern inventions of railroads, steamships, and refrigerated cars to carry produce, and its pests, to ever-more-distant places. For these reasons, the late nineteenth century was a time of insect plagues.

Boll weevils came over the border from Mexico and did huge harm to cotton in the American South. The elm leaf beetle came from

(left)
A boy mixes road dust with Paris Green, whose main ingredients were poisonous arsenic and copper.

Europe and ravaged elm trees in U.S. cities. Later a pest from Asia, misleadingly called Dutch elm disease, would wipe out almost every elm east of the Mississippi. An Australian insect called the cottony cushion scale swept through California's citrus industry. An American insect called phylloxera wrecked vineyards in most of France and Italy.

In 1875, at the height of the Colorado potato beetle crisis, the *New York Times* called for "an aggressive war upon the beetles." But war with what weapon? Farmers tried everything they could think of, from crushing the beetles with special pincers to spraying tobacco juice and even kerosene on their fields. Nothing worked. Then someone discovered that Paris Green, the material that gave an emerald color to paint, killed Colorado potato beetles. Paris Green had been developed in the late eighteenth century and was common in paints, fabrics, and wallpapers. Farmers began buying it, mixing it with flour or water, and dusting or sprinkling it on their potato plants—then watching the beetles die.

The main ingredients in Paris Green are

arsenic and copper. Inspired by the success of Paris Green against potato beetles, the rising chemical industry looked into attacking other agricultural problems with these chemicals and others. In the mid-1880s a French researcher found that a compound known as copper sulfate would kill downy mildew on grapevines. Researchers tried it on other pests and discovered, to their joy, that it killed the potato blight that had caused the Great Hunger. Spraying potatoes with Paris Green and then copper sulfate would get rid of both beetle and blight. The pesticide industry, devoted to manufacturing chemicals to kill or prevent pests, had been born.

From the beginning, farmers knew that both Paris Green and copper sulfate were toxic. Many people had gotten sick from living in homes with wallpaper printed with Paris Green. The arsenic it contains is a strong poison. The thought of spraying food with poison made farmers anxious. They feared letting it build up in the soil, and they worried about exposing themselves and their workers to dangerous chemicals. For a long time, though, farmers didn't know about the most troubling issue of all: that the chemicals would stop working.

A Steady Stream of Chemicals

Colorado potato beetles adapt quickly to new circumstances. As early as 1912 a few of them showed signs of being immune to Paris Green. Farmers didn't notice, however, because the pesticide industry kept coming up with new arsenic mixtures that kept killing potato beetles. After the middle of the twentieth century, a new type of pesticide was introduced. It was DDT, a bug killer more effective than any that had come before. Farmers bought DDT and cheered as insects vanished from their fields.

The celebration lasted about seven years. The Colorado potato beetle adapted and developed resistance to DDT. Potato growers demanded new chemicals. By the mid-1980s, each new pesticide in the eastern United States was good for about a season.

Potato farmers now treat their crops a dozen or more times a season with an ever-changing stream of deadly substances. In addition, they treat the crops with artificial fertilizer, usually

(right)
As this 1877 illustration suggests, British farmers feared the arrival of the Colorado potato beetle.

once a week during growing season. Critics of pesticides call this a "toxic treadmill." Large-scale potato farmers douse their land with so many chemicals that the fields are swept free of all life except for the potato plants. If rain doesn't fall for a few days, the powders and liquids can build up on the soil surface so that it looks like the aftermath of a chemical-warfare test. I have met farmers who claimed not to allow their children to walk in their fields. You don't have to be an organic food fanatic to wonder about a system that turns the growing of food into a toxic act.

Worse still, many researchers believe that the chemical assault does more harm than good. Strong pesticides kill not just the pests they're aimed at but other insect species as well, including insects that are the natural enemies of the pests. When the pest species develop resistance and survive the chemicals, they are often better off than before, because everything that had once limited their numbers is gone. In this way pesticides can actually increase the number of harmful insects unless farmers control them with still more chemical weapons.

In 2008 a research team announced in the *American Journal of Potato Research* that new chemicals were on the way but that these new products were unlikely to break the cycle of pesticide, followed by resistance, followed by a new pesticide. The researchers admitted, "Despite all the scientific and technological advances, the Colorado potato beetle continues to be a major threat to potato production."

Potato blight has returned, too. In 1981 Swiss researchers were dismayed to discover that a second type of *P. infestans*, formerly known only in Mexico, had found its way to Europe. It has more genetic diversity than the version that killed Europe's potatoes in the nineteenth century, which means that it has more resources for adapting and developing resistance to chemicals. This strain of blight has also appeared in the United States. It is more destructive than the first strain, and more resistant to the chemical that is now the main antiblight treatment. No good substitute for that chemical has been found.

In 2009, as I was writing the first draft

of this book, potato blight wiped out most of the potatoes and tomatoes on the East Coast of the United States. Driven by an unusually wet summer, it turned gardens all around me into slime and bare stalks. It destroyed the few tomatoes in my garden that had not been drowned by rain.

PART FOUR: EUROPE IN THE WORLD

CHAPTER 8

WEALTH THAT GREW ON TREES

NEAR THE VILLAGE OF LONGYIN LE, IN southern China, I walked through something that I couldn't name. It looked just like a forest, but ecologists probably wouldn't call it one. To be sure, it was full of graceful fifty-foot-tall trees. Yet every one of the trees was the same species, the Pará rubber tree, and they were planted in straight rows. All were the same age. They had been put in the soil forty-five years before. Every other plant species that grew higher than my ankles had been cleared away.

The driver of the cab that had brought me to Longyin Le walked with me. He said he had not been to this area since he was young. The hills had been full of mammals and birds then. Now the hills were silent. Except for a few plants and mosses, every living thing that I could see was a rubber tree.

When the bark of a rubber tree is cut, a milky goo called latex seeps out. Depending on the tree and the season, as much as 90 percent of the latex is water. Some of the rest of it consists of tiny grains of natural rubber, a major industrial product that is greatly desired by manufacturers of high technology. The forest outside Longyin Le was a rubber plantation, one of many.

More than a century ago, a handful of Pará rubber trees came to Asia from their home in Brazil. Now the descendants of those trees carpet sections of the Philippines, Indonesia, Malaysia, Thailand, and China, and they are marching into Laos and Vietnam. A plant that before Columbus had never existed outside the Amazon now dominates ecosystems in Southeast Asia.

Rubber reigns over such a wide area that botanists warn that a single epidemic of plant disease—something like the potato blight described in chapter 7—could lead to an ecological calamity. Also, because rubber is a vitally important resource in the modern industrial world, that ecological calamity could cause a worldwide economic breakdown.

Just as the potato helped bring about the

(*left*)
Guide strips for latex and collection cups mark this rubber plantation in China near the Laos border.

Agricultural Revolution, rubber helped bring about the Industrial Revolution, which was the shift from an economy based on human and animal labor to one based on mechanized manufacturing. Along the way the rubber tree was entwined with the lives of countless men and women: unfortunate slaves, visionary engineers, hungry merchants, obsessed scientists, and empire-building politicians. That forest of alien trees outside Longyin Le was the work of many hands in many places, and it was much older than forty-five years.

A New Form of Matter

In 1526 a group of Indians from Mexico played a ball game in Spain for the entertainment of the Spanish royal court and its guests. The Indians were former citizens of the Aztec Empire, conquered by the conquistador Hernán Cortés just five years before. The game was *ullamaliztli*, in which two teams of players compete to drive fist-size balls through hoops on opposite ends of the field.

The ambassador from Venice saw the game and was fascinated by the balls. Unlike European game balls, which were made of leather and

Auf Solches mamer spilen die
Judianer mit ainem aufgeblassen
bal mit dem hindert. On die Hend
an die Rieren auf der Erdt.
haben auch ain handt leder for dem
hindern dar mit er vom bal den
widerstraeig. Entpfaeht haben
auch solich leder hent
schueh an

(top)
Europeans were
fascinated by the *ul-
lamaliztli* ballplayers
who toured Spain
in the 1520s—and
by the rubber ball,
which was unlike
anything ever seen
in Europe.

(left)
Rubber shoes made
in Brazil for the
American market,
probably in the
1830s.

stuffed with wool or feathers, the Mexican balls "bounded copiously," he wrote. A witness at another game marveled that whenever the balls touched the ground, even lightly, they sprang into the air "with the most incredible leaps."

Europeans were puzzled by these bouncing balls. They were right to be puzzled, because they were seeing a form of matter that was entirely new to them. The *ullamaliztli* balls were made of rubber. Chemists use the term elastomers for the group of materials that includes rubber. The name refers to the elastic properties of these materials—that is, their ability to stretch and bounce. No Europeans had seen elastomers before the Columbian Exchange.

Even though Europeans were impressed by rubber's bounciness, they did not immediately realize its potential. Serious studies of rubber did not begin until the 1740s. In 1805 a scientist named John Gough performed the first simple laboratory experiments on it. These experiments gave little hint that rubber might be useful, although Gough did discover that rubber heats up when it is stretched and shrinks when it is heated. Not until the 1820s did rubber really take off for Europeans and Americans, with the invention of the waterproof boots known as galoshes.

Indians in South America had been using rubber for centuries, perhaps for thousands of years. They milked rubber trees by slashing V-shaped cuts into the trunk. Latex dripped from the point of the V into a container, usually a hollow gourd, mounted below the cut. To obtain rubber from the latex, the Indians slowly boiled it and stretched it over fires, then shaped it into stiff pipes, dishes, and other useful objects. They may also have waterproofed their hats and cloaks by soaking the cloth in liquid latex.

By the late eighteenth century, European colonists in the Amazon were making rubberized garments. They made boots by dipping foot-shaped molds into bubbling pots of latex. When a few pairs of these boots made their way to the United States, they were a big hit. Cities such as Boston, Philadelphia, and Washington, DC, were built on swamps. Their streets were thick with mud, and there were no sidewalks. Waterproof footwear seemed like a fantastic idea.

The center of "rubber fever" was Salem, north of Boston. In 1825 a young Salem businessman

imported five hundred pairs of rubber shoes from Brazil. Ten years later, the number of imported shoes had grown to four hundred thousand pairs, about one for every forty Americans. Rubber shoes were modern, high-tech, and exciting—the perfect urban accessory. People flocked to stores to buy them.

Then came the crash. The idea of waterproof rubber boots, it turned out, was more exciting than the reality. Pure rubber footwear simply didn't work very well. In cold weather the shoes became brittle and stiff. In hot weather they melted. Boots left in closets at the end of one winter turned into black puddles by the beginning of the next. Rubber dealers were swamped with returned merchandise. Public opinion swung violently against rubber.

Jail Cells and a Rolling Pin

Just before the collapse of the galoshes boom, a bankrupt businessman named Charles Goodyear became obsessed by rubber. He declared that he was going to find a way to make it stable, so that it would keep its shape and stretchiness at all temperatures. A few weeks later, he was thrown into prison for his debts.

(left)
Who invented vulcanization, making rubber usable for industry? Charles Goodyear had the idea first but never fully understood the process.

That didn't stop Goodyear. In his cell he began work, mashing bits of rubber with a rolling pin. The fact that he knew nothing of chemistry didn't squelch his boundless enthusiasm.

Goodyear got out of prison and spent years wandering around the northeastern United States, trailed by his hungry wife and children and dodging bill collectors. All the while he was mixing toxic chemicals, more or less at random, hoping to find a combination that would make rubber stable. At various times, the Goodyears lived in abandoned rubber factories or in houses with no heat or food.

Acting on a tip from another rubber obsessive, Goodyear began mixing rubber with sulfur. Then, one day, he accidentally dropped a lump of sulfur-treated rubber onto a hot stove and saw, to his amazement, that the rubber didn't melt. The surface charred, but the inside changed into a new kind of rubber, one that kept its shape and stretchiness at a high temperature. He threw himself into trying to reproduce the accident. This task was made more challenging by the need to traipse from neighbor to neighbor to use their woodstoves. Over the years, in and out of prison for debt, Goodyear kept working.

Along the way he befriended a young Englishman and gave him some successful samples of sulfur-treated rubber. In 1842 two small strips of Goodyear's rubber ended up in the laboratory of an English engineer named Thomas Hancock, who had already developed some processes for working with rubber. Hancock had no idea where the samples originated, but he saw that they didn't melt in hot weather or become stiff in cold weather. He set out to achieve the same results.

After a year and a half of systematic experiments, Hancock, who was more knowledgeable and better organized than Goodyear, learned that soaking rubber in melted sulfur turned it into something that kept its shape and stretchiness in all weather. Later he called this process "vulcanization," after Vulcan, the Roman god of fire. The British government granted Hancock a patent for his process on May 21, 1844.

Three weeks later, the U.S. government granted Goodyear his vulcanization patent. Goodyear's patent application shows that he never fully understood the process, but he did realize that at last he had a business opportunity.

In spite of receiving some recognition, however, Goodyear was still awash in debt when he died in 1860.

Molecules Like Spaghetti

It was not until the twentieth century that chemists began to understand why sulfur stabilized rubber, or even why rubber bounced and stretched. Rubber and other elastomers have molecules shaped like long chains. (If a rubber molecule were as thick as a pencil, it would be as long as a football field.) These chains are scrambled around one another in no clear pattern, like noodles in a bowl of spaghetti. Stretching a rubber band pulls the tangled molecules into lines, like strands of uncooked spaghetti in a box. When rubber is stretched, the molecules unkink as they go from a tangled snarl to their full length. When the pressure is relaxed, the molecules begin moving randomly again, and the rubber shrinks back to its original size.

If a lump of pure rubber is heated, the molecules slither around and get even more disordered, and the rubber melts into a puddle. Vulcanization with sulfur builds chemical

(*left*)
Thomas Hancock patented the process first and understood it better, but was likely inspired by Goodyear.

bonds that act like bridges linking the rubber molecules together. Once linked, the molecules can't readily relax into a snarl, even when heated. Rubber suddenly becomes a stable material.

Vulcanization had a profound impact on industrial development. It made possible the inflated rubber tire, which was key to the large-scale use of bicycles and automobiles. Rubber also made electrification possible by insulating electrical wires. In appliances such as washers and dryers, and in countless other machines, belts made of rubber transfer the energy of engines to the moving parts. Furnaces and the internal combustion engines of automobiles work safely and smoothly because flexible rubber washers, gaskets, and rings keep liquids and gases from leaking.

The Industrial Revolution needed three basic materials: steel, fossil fuels such as coal and oil, and rubber. The rapidly industrializing nations of Europe and North America had steel and fossil fuels in abundance. They needed to secure a supply of rubber.

RUBBER ROOMS

CHARLES GOODYEAR, ONE OF THE INVENTORS
of the vulcanizing process for making rubber
stable and usable, struggled with debt to the end
of his life. Still, he had a knack for publicity stunts.
Once he had received a patent for his vulcanizing
process, he wanted to promote it. He spent thirty
thousand dollars he did not have to create an
entire room made of rubber for the first world's
fair, the Great Exhibition of 1851, in London. Four
years later he borrowed another fifty thousand
dollars to create an even more lavish rubber room
at the second world's fair, in Paris.

Parisians lost their urban cool and gawped
at Goodyear's rubber dressing table, complete
with rubber-framed mirror and a battalion of
rubber combs. In the center of the rubber floor
was a hard rubber desk with a rubber inkwell and
rubber pens. Rubber umbrellas stood at attention
in a rubber umbrella stand in a corner formed by

By mixing rubber
with sulfur, Good-
year learned how to
make it weather-re-
sistant and good for
all seasons—and all
styles, as shown in
this late nineteenth-
century poster.

two rubber walls; on each wall hung paintings on rubber canvases. For weapons fans, there was a stand of knives in rubber sheaths, swords in rubber scabbards, and rifles with rubber stocks.

Except for the unpleasant rubber smell, Goodyear's Paris exhibition was a triumph. Napoléon III, the French emperor, awarded Goodyear the Legion of Honor. Yet Goodyear's money troubles soon caught up with him. A Paris court sent him to prison for debt, and he received his Legion of Honor medal while sitting in his jail cell. Goodyear had to sell some of his wife's possessions to pay for their trip home to the United States.

My Ancestor in the Amazon

In my living room hangs a portrait of either my grandmother's uncle or her great-great-uncle. Both men were named Neville Burgoyne Craig. The nineteenth-century style of the painting makes me think it is a portrait of her uncle, who lived from 1847 to 1926. He was an engineer who sailed for the Amazon a week after his thirty-first birthday, planning to make his fortune in rubber.

Craig was not going to work directly with rubber. Instead, he intended to help build a railroad to carry it. In his time the primary source of natural rubber was the Pará rubber tree, as it still is. Native to the Amazon Basin, this tree is most abundant on the borderlands between Brazil and Bolivia. The ports nearest to this area are on the Pacific coast, west across the forbidding Andes Mountains. A longer but less challenging and less expensive way to get rubber to market was to send it east, down the Madeira River, which flows into the Amazon River, and then down the Amazon to the Atlantic. There was just one problem. Waterfalls and violent rapids blocked a 229-mile stretch of the Madeira.

My ancestor went to Brazil to build a railroad through the rainforest around the rapids.

According to a memoir that Craig later wrote, the venture ran into trouble from the start. One of two ships carrying engineers and laborers from Philadelphia to Brazil was wrecked by storms. Craig was aboard the ship that made it. He steamed up the Amazon to the site where the planned railway was to end, only to have a problem with Italian laborers who went on strike because they had discovered they were being paid less than other workers. Craig and other engineers made a cage from the steel rails for the railway and forced the striking workers into it at gunpoint. (Craig did not seem to worry that imprisoning his workforce might slow down the construction schedule.)

Eventually the strikers went back to work, sullenly hacking at the trees. A few weeks later, some seventy-five of them fled into the forest. They were never seen again. The expedition itself, meanwhile, was running out of food. Like the Jamestown colonists discussed in chapter 3, the railroad builders were starving in the midst of plenty because they did not know where to fish or how to use local food sources, such as palm fruits.

(*left*)
Neville B. Craig

What finally capsized the venture was malaria. Within a few months, three-fourths of the crew were too sick to work. Many died. After my ancestor had been in the Amazon for about a year, the venture reached what he called "complete collapse." Sick and broke, shoeless and ragged, Craig and a hundred or so other survivors straggled down the Amazon River to a port where they could beg passage home. Even as they haunted the docks, though, masters of finance in Europe and America were already planning another shot at building the railroad. There was too much money in rubber to let the idea go.

A Big Boom

Even in a time of crazy boom-and-bust cycles, the rubber boom stood out. Brazil's rubber exports grew more than ten times between 1856 and 1896, then by four more times by 1912. Ordinarily such an enormous increase in production would drive down prices, but the price of rubber kept climbing. In 1910 the *New York Times* declared, "One ounce of rubber, washed and prepared for manufacture, is worth nearly its weight in pure silver."

(*top right*)
Rubber World,
c. 1890.

(*bottom right*)
At the peak of the rubber boom, a Brazilian survey found hundreds of rubber-processing facilities on the banks of the Purus River, a tributary of the Amazon.

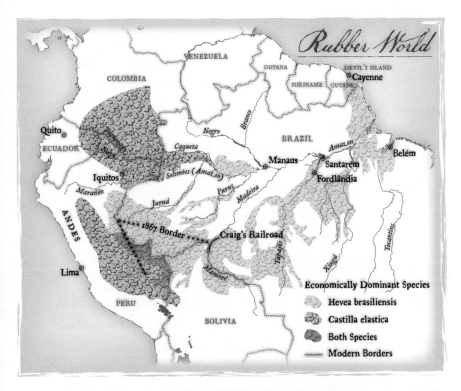

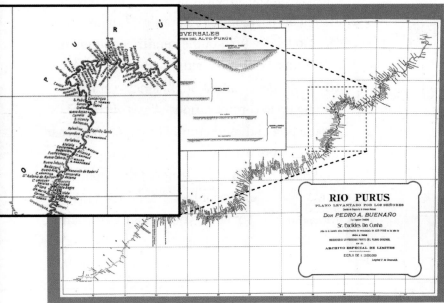

The financial center of the rubber trade was the Brazilian city of Belém, at the entrance to the Amazon River. The city's newly rich rubber elite lined the cobblestone streets with European-style cafés, parks, and mansions. Rubber was everywhere, wrote a visitor in 1911, "on the sidewalks, in the streets, on trucks, in the great storehouses, and in the air—that is, the smell of it."

Almost a thousand miles inland, another city on the great river was the center of rubber collection. Manaus was not just one of the most remote cities on earth but also one of the richest. It sprawled across four hills, with stone sidewalks, a ridiculously expensive opera house made of imported marble, and one of the world's most advanced streetcar networks. Filled with bordellos, barrooms, and brawls, Manaus was the model of a turn-of-the-century boomtown.

All that wealth—wealth that literally grew on trees—attracted attention. Business ventures sprang up to control various stages of rubber production and marketing. The export houses in Manaus were usually run by Europeans. These middlemen unloaded and stored the rubber that came from the interior before sending it to the mouth of the Amazon, where other European-run merchant houses shipped it to Europe and North America. As for the rubber itself, it was obtained by another group of businesses that controlled the most vital resource in the interior of the Amazon Basin: human beings.

Getting rubber from trees took a lot of work. Tappers, the workers who took the latex from the trees, had to make fresh cuts in each tree daily during the four- to five-month tapping season. They then had to process the latex into crude rubber before it dried and became difficult to work with. All this took place in remote, malaria-ridden forest camps. Disease and slaving raids had harshly cut back the native population, so the ever-greater hunger for rubber was matched by an ever-more-desperate shortage of workers. Some of the solutions that emerged were beastly.

At first the rubber boom seemed like a godsend to the always-poor people of the region, but things soon took a darker turn. Rubber estates hired local Indians, shipped in penniless farmers from downriver, or kidnapped workers from Bolivia. Laborers were housed in barren dormitories patrolled by armed guards, to keep workers from running away. Deeper in the interior, rubber was obtained by simply cutting down and draining a different species of rubber tree. There, warlord-like men from Peru and Brazil used violence and armies of thugs to control sprawling private rubber empires worked by thousands of indigenous slaves. One of the worst abusers was Julio César Arana, the son of a Peruvian hatmaker. He set up a company in London as a front for his Amazonian empire. Investigations by journalists and by the British government eventually brought an end to these brutal enterprises.

Other forces took different approaches to building their own rubber empires. Political and business leaders in Europe and the United States were furious that rubber, so vital to their economies, was completely controlled by South America. From Brazil's point of view, the greatest threat was the United States. As early as the 1850s some Americans had claimed that the United States should take control of the Amazon Basin. That scheme came to nothing, and Brazil tightened its control over rubber. Brazil wanted to keep its monopoly on rubber—in other words, it wanted to remain the only source of this increasingly important resource. It failed, thanks to a man who became an agent of the Columbian Exchange.

The Tree Thief

Henry Alexander Wickham has been called a thief and a patriot, a major figure in industrial history, and a hapless dolt who failed in businesses on three continents. Born in England in 1846, Wickham spent his life trying to improve his social and financial status by growing tropical plants on plantations from Central America to Australia. His ventures wrecked his marriage and drove away his family, yet at the end of his days Wickham was a respected man, having received a knighthood for an exploit he undertook in 1876.

In the early 1870s, an official in the British government let it be known that Britain would pay for rubber seeds. This was not the first quest for a "forbidden" tree. Years earlier, that same official had masterminded a successful plan to smuggle seedlings of the cinchona tree out of South America, where governments closely guarded them. Cinchona bark was the source of the drug quinine, which was then the only effective medicine for treating malaria. The nations of Peru, Ecuador, and Bolivia wanted to preserve their monopoly on cinchona, but they were killing the trees by stripping their bark. Transplanted to

India, the smuggled seedlings became cinchona plantations that saved thousands of lives.

In response to the call for rubber seeds, two hopeful adventurers sent batches of seeds to London. Neither batch would sprout. Wickham was the third to try. His base of operations was his failing manioc plantation in Santarém, Brazil. The area had been settled by a number of Confederate families who had fled the American South for South America after the Civil War. With the help of some of these families, Wickham gathered seventy thousand rubber seeds and took them to London. Fewer than three thousand sprouted there—but they were enough. Shipped to Asia, the seedlings that sprouted from Wickham's seeds were the beginning of rubber plantations in Sri Lanka, Malaysia, and Indonesia.

In 1897, Sri Lanka and Malaysia had a thousand acres of rubber plantations. Fifteen years later, rubber covered six hundred fifty thousand acres. For the first time, more rubber came from Asia than from South America. Prices fell, and the Brazilian rubber industry was reduced to dust. The opera house in Manaus closed its doors, and the city's mansions were abandoned.

(*left*)
Henry Wickham.

"BIO-PIRACY" OR BENEFIT?

THE RUBBER SEEDS THAT HENRY WICKHAM
smuggled out of South America gave birth to
the vast rubber plantations of Asia. Although
Wickham received a British knighthood for his
feat, he is regarded with scorn and loathing
in Brazil. Tourist guides call him a "prince of
thieves" and a pioneer of "bio-piracy," the
stealing of biological resources.

Brazil had no bio-piracy laws in the nineteenth
century. In addition, there is no evidence that
anyone tried to stop Wickham. The British

government's call for rubber seeds was hardly
a secret. It had been trumpeted in London
newspapers. Besides, Brazilians themselves had
not hesitated to adopt foreign plant and animal
species. Brazil's primary agricultural exports today
are soybeans, beef, sugar, and coffee. Not one of
them is native to the Americas. The first coffee
seeds in Brazil, in fact, were smuggled into the
country by one of the nation's diplomats.

Taking useful species beyond their home
environments has been, on balance, a good thing
for humankind. The supply of quinine in the Andes
was far too small to treat the world's malaria
sufferers. Carrying it to Asia and Africa prevented
many premature deaths. Transplanting the potato
to Europe and the sweet potato to China created
catastrophic social and environmental problems,
as shown in chapters 6 and 7, but the tubers
also kept millions of Europeans and Chinese
from malnutrition and famine. To date, the huge
benefits of moving species outweigh the huge
harms, although the story is still being told.

A young boy with
rubber ready to be
shipped, in late
nineteenth-century
India.

"Diseases Always Come In"

In the late 1920s the American inventor and businessman Henry Ford, who was then the world's most important automobile maker, attempted to start his own rubber plantation on land he bought in Brazil. The settlement he built to house his workers looked just like a middle-class Michigan town, complete with movie theaters and bungalows on tree-lined streets. On a nearby hilltop was the Amazon's only golf course. Fordlândia, as people soon began calling the place, was orderly and straitlaced, the opposite of boomtown Manaus.

Within a few years, Ford's tidy venture ran into problems. One problem was erosion, from cutting down the forest to build the town on hills. Another was that the company did not find out until after the first season's rubber trees had died that the trees had to be planted at certain times of the year. The biggest problem, though, was a fungus called *Microcyclus ulei*, which is partial to rubber trees.

M. ulei causes South American leaf blight. When a spore of the fungus lands on the leaf of a rubber tree, it grows, spreads, and then drills into the leaf. It produces many more spores, which come out from tubes that the fungus forms on the bottom of the leaf. These new spores are knocked free by raindrops or brushed off when leaves rub together. Left behind are ruined, blackened leaves, which fall off the tree. Many rubber trees survive a bout with *M. ulei*, but their growth is stunted. A second or third attack of the fungus will kill them.

Rubber trees in the wild are usually spaced far apart—that's one reason harvesting wild latex is such difficult work. The large distance between the trees means that if one tree falls to leaf blight, other trees will be too far away to be attacked by the spores, which die soon after parting from the leaf. In plantations, however, the trees are planted so close together that their upper branches are entangled. Spores hop from tree to tree like squirrels, or are carried on the clothes or under the fingernails of plantation workers. That's what happened in Fordlândia.

Ford's plant scientist had imported rubber tree buds from Indonesia, where planters had developed a variety that produced a higher-than-normal amount of latex. Unfortunately, this variety also had a lower-than-normal resistance to *M. ulei*. Soon Fordlândia's plantations were

Almost every bit of this south China region that can support rubber trees has been cleared and planted, sucking up the area's water supply. Running out of suitable land in China, Chinese rubber companies have moved into northern Laos.

285

overrun by leaf blight, and the venture was abandoned in 1945.

During World War II (1939–1945) industrial chemists learned how to mass-produce synthetic, or artificial, rubber. Even today, though, synthetic rubber does not equal natural rubber's durability, stability, or flexibility. Natural rubber still claims more than 40 percent of the market. With its need for materials that can withstand battle conditions, the military is a major consumer of rubber—which is why the United States banned the sale of natural rubber to China when the two nations came into conflict in the Korean War of the 1950s. China decided to grow its own rubber, although only the extreme southern tip of the country is warm enough for rubber trees. Since the 1990s, China has been investing in rubber plantations in the neighboring Southeast Asian nations of Laos and Myanmar (Burma).

Rubber trees suck great quantities of water from the ground. Ecologists have noted that the rise of rubber plantations in southernmost China and the area known as the Golden Triangle (where Laos, Myanmar, and Thailand meet) has been matched by the drying-up of streams and the erosion of soil. Even if planters stopped planting rubber trees tomorrow, however, the trees would continue on their own to invade the forest around them.

The great majority of the rubber trees in Southeast Asia are clones, like the potatoes in the United States when the Colorado potato beetle arrived. The rubber trees were grafted from the wood of specimens that produced a lot of latex. Grafted trees are genetically identical to their sources. Most of those sources are descended from the survivors of Henry Wickham's expedition. They represent a tiny slice of the genetic variability of the wild rubber tree.

Monoculture rubber plantations are less resistant to disease than a more genetically mixed population of trees would be. As the area of rubber cultivation grows larger, it becomes an increasingly inviting target for pests. "That's the lesson of biology," says Chinese ecologist Tang Jianwei. "Diseases always come in. Sooner or later, they'll find a way."

For a century, the rubber plantations have been saved by their isolation. Southeast Asia was isolated from Brazil, and the Southeast Asian nations were isolated from one another. Now, though, the world is knitting itself together ever more closely. If *M. ulei* makes it to Asia from Brazil, a new highway can carry it swiftly between Cambodia, Laos, Myanmar, Thailand, and China. Tang estimates that an outbreak of South American leaf blight could wipe out Asia's rubber trees in ten to twenty years.

The disaster would take a long time to repair. Natural rubber is vital to many aspects of modern life. Imagine airplanes and large trucks without tires, hospitals without sterile rubber hoses or gloves, electric power plants without gaskets or seals. Plant breeders are working on new varieties of rubber trees that will resist *M. ulei*, but progress is slow. If a problem occurs, the cycle of the Columbian Exchange will be complete: a fungus from Brazil will reach Asia, where it will wipe out the Asian trees that originated in Brazil. The epidemic will cover an area large enough to be seen from space—blackened splotches from the tip of China to the end of Indonesia. Nations will pull together to fight the outbreak, and planters will suddenly be aware that they are living in a time when Asia and the Americas are growing more and more alike.

De Chami
sale Cambu
india 2. c

PART FIVE

AFRICA IN THE WORLD

ndia.
amizo 1.
ja 3.

UNTIL AROUND 1700, ABOUT 90 PERCENT OF the people who crossed the Atlantic Ocean were African captives. Because of this great shift in human populations, for three centuries the majority groups in many American landscapes were Africans, indigenous Indians, and mixed-race Afro-Indians. They interacted in ways long hidden from Europeans. Those interrelationships, brought about by the Columbian Exchange, are an important part of history.

The meeting of Africans and American Indians took place against a backdrop of other meetings. Columbus's voyage set off a spasm of migrations that involved many different peoples. The world's first multilanguage, world-encompassing metropolis arose in Mexico City. Its cultural jumble extended from the top, where the Spanish conquistadors married into the royal families of the Indians they had conquered, to the bottom, where Spanish barbers complained about immigrant barbers from China. Mexico City, which connected the networks of Atlantic and Pacific journeys that made up the Columbian Exchange, was a true planetary crossroads. It was the scene of cultural, economic, and racial exchanges that continue in our globalized world today.

CHAPTER 9

CRAZY SOUP

FOR THOUSANDS OF YEARS, ALMOST ALL
Europeans were found in Europe. Few Africans
existed outside Africa. Nearly all Asians lived
in Asia. Columbus's voyages launched a
reshuffling of *Homo sapiens*, the human part of
the Columbian Exchange. People shot around
the world like dice flung on a gaming table.
Europeans became the majority in Argentina
and Australia. Africans were found from South
America to Seattle. Chinatowns sprang up all
over the globe.

This worldwide reshuffling of the human
species was dominated by the African slave
trade. For a long time, the scale of slavery in the
Americas was not fully grasped. According to a
2009 estimate, based on an international study
of more than thirty-five thousand separate slave

voyages, 11.7 million captives left Africa for the Americas between 1500 and 1840. In that same period, perhaps 3.4 Europeans immigrated to the Americas. Roughly speaking, for every European who came to the Americas, three Africans made the trip.

These figures mean that the common picture of American history is wrong.

Generations of textbooks presented American history as Europeans moving into a lightly settled hemisphere. In fact, the hemisphere was full of tens of millions of indigenous peoples. Most of the movement into the hemisphere was by Africans, who soon became the majority population in almost every place that wasn't controlled by Indians. As one researcher of the slave trade has written, "America was an extension of Africa rather than Europe until late in the nineteenth century."

In the three centuries after Columbus's voyages, migrants from across the Atlantic came to the Americas. They built new cities and filled them with houses, churches, taverns, stables, and more. They cleared forests, planted fields, laid out roads, and tended horses, cattle, and sheep—animals that had not walked the

Americas before. They reworked the American landscape, creating a new world that was an ecological and cultural mix.

This great transformation was a turning point in the history of our species. It was carried out largely by African hands. The crowds thronging the streets in the new cities were mainly African. The farmers growing wheat and rice in the new farms were mainly African. The men and women on boats and in mills and gardens and plantations were mainly African.

An even larger wave of migration arrived from Europe in the nineteenth century, changing the demographic balance of the Americas once again. Europeans and their descendants became the majority in most of the hemisphere. Surrounded by people like them, they did not often realize they were following trails that had been set for more than three hundred years by Africans.

The human Columbian Exchange broke the geographic barriers that had largely kept Europeans, Africans, Asians, and Americans apart for so long. The Atlantic slave trade was the first wave of that human exchange, and the force that drove it was sugar.

Haitian children carry sugarcane across a field in Port-au-Prince, 2010.

297

A Taste for Sweetness

Sugarcane was first domesticated in New Guinea, north of Australia, about ten thousand years ago. About half the plant, by weight, consists of sucrose, a sweet, grainy substance known as table sugar or cane sugar. Scientists debate among themselves whether sucrose is actually addictive or people just act like it is. Either way, it has been an amazingly powerful force in human affairs. Unlike a taste for salt or spice, a sweet tooth seems to be present in every culture and every part of the world.

From its home in New Guinea, sugar spread north and west, into China and India. By AD 800 the Islamic peoples of the Middle East were irrigating sugarcane plantations in what is now Lebanon and Israel. Europeans encountered sugarcane when they conquered that region in 1096, during the First Crusade.

At the time, sugar was quite rare in Europe. Like Asian spices such as ginger and pepper, it was found only in the kitchens of a few princes and nobles. The crusaders began exporting sugar to Europe, feeding an appetite for sweetness. Sugarcane plantations appeared in the few parts of southern Europe that were

(*top right*)
Spread of Sugar Through the Mediterrranean and Beyond

(*bottom right*)
Sugar mills were smoky, steamy places that required many workers, as shown in this engraving of a Sicilian mill around 1600.

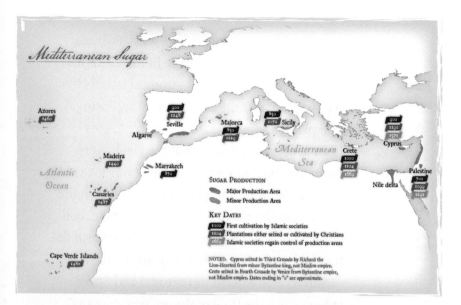

Mediterranean Sugar

Azores
1460

Seville
900
1248

Algarve

Majorca
850
1229

Sicily
850
1072

Cyprus
900
1190
1571

Crete
1000
1204
1669

Palestine
700
1099
1291

Nile delta

Madeira
1440

Marrakech
870

Atlantic
Ocean

Canaries
1437

Mediterranean
Sea

Cape Verde Islands
1450

SUGAR PRODUCTION

Major Production Area

Minor Production Area

KEY DATES

1000 First cultivation by Islamic societies
1204 Plantations either seized or cultivated by Christians
1669 Islamic societies regain control of production areas

NOTES: Cyprus seized in Third Crusade by Richard the
Lion-Hearted from minor Byzantine king, not Muslim empire.
Crete seized in Fourth Crusade by Venice from Byzantine empire,
not Muslim empire. Dates ending in "o" are approximate.

warm and wet enough. Before long, Portugal and Spain were growing cane in the Canaries, Cape Verde, and Madeira—tropical islands in the Atlantic near the coast of Africa. (Portugal also planted some sugarcane in the Azores Islands off its own coast, but the yields were disappointing because the climate was too cold.)

Sugar boomed, but plantation owners on the island colonies needed labor to slash cane, boil down the juice into sugar, and pack and load the finished product. For this they turned to slaves.

Slavery had existed in Portugal and Spain at least since the time of the ancient Romans, but the nature of slavery on the sugarcane plantations was different. At first the labor force was drawn from convicts, the local native population, and prisoners of war, but when sugarcane growers began buying large numbers of captive Africans, plantation slavery was born.

In the 1560s and 1570s, a flood of sugar from big new plantations in the Americas swept away the competition from the Atlantic islands. As early as 1523, Hernán Cortés, the Spanish conqueror of Mexico, had begun growing cane on his huge estate south of Mexico City. Plantation owners in the Americas faced the

same need for labor. In Spain's American
colonies, the labor question was tied to the
question of how the Indians should be treated.

Unfree Indians, Enslaved Africans
The official position of the Spanish crown and
the Roman Catholic Church was that conquering
the Indians was acceptable if it was done with
the goal of making them into Christians. The
Spaniards who actually went to the new colonies
in the Americas, though, were more interested in
Indian labor than in Indian souls.

The Crown found itself in a dilemma. On one
hand, the justification for conquest was that the
Indians were to be converted to Christianity,
which was not likely to happen if large numbers
of them were enslaved. On the other hand,
the colonies were also supposed to contribute
to the glory and wealth of Spain, and for that
they needed a labor force. The solution was the
encomienda system, which was introduced in
1503 and later modified several times. Under
this system, individual Spanish conquistadors
became the guardians or trustees of Indian
groups, promising to ensure their safety,
freedom, and religious instruction. The Indians

paid for this Spanish "security" with their labor.

The *encomienda* system was supposed to limit the demands that the conquistadors could make on the Indians, which would make the Indians less likely to revolt against Spanish rule. It didn't work. Both the Indians and the conquistadors disliked the system. Under the law, the Indians were still free people, with their towns and villages governed by their own leaders. In reality, the leaders had little power and the Indians were often treated as slaves. They were not officially enslaved, but they were not truly free.

Cortés may have had more unfree Indians (more than twenty thousand of them) than anyone else in the world. Many labored on his estate's sugarcane plantations. In 1542 the Spanish Crown officially banned enslavement of Indians, and the trend was clear. Although there were loopholes in the new law, it was going to become harder for Spanish conquistadors and colonists to force Indians to work for them. A few weeks after the new antislavery law was announced, Cortés made a deal with an Italian merchant to buy five hundred Africans whom he could legally own and force to work. When the first hundred captives were delivered two years later, the Atlantic slave trade had arrived.

Africans had been trickling into the Americas almost as long as Europeans had been. Remains found in the cemetery of Columbus's colony La Isabela suggest that some of the settlers there were of African descent. Once Africans were brought to Hispaniola to work on sugarcane plantations, escaped slaves became a serious problem for the Spanish colony. Hidden by the forest, these roaming Africans made it their business to wreck the sugar industry that had enchained them.

In the second half of the sixteenth century, the center of the Spanish sugar industry shifted to mainland Mexico. Sugar production soared. No longer were Africans slipped into the Americas by the handful. The rise of plantation agriculture in Mexico and in Portugal's Brazilian colony opened the floodgates. Between 1550 and 1650, slave ships ferried across about six hundred fifty thousand Africans to Spanish and Portuguese America. In those places, African immigrants outnumbered European immigrants by more than two to one—with results the Europeans never expected.

Africans walked with the Spanish conquistadors, sometimes as soldiers, sometimes as servants or slaves. They poured by the thousands into Peru and Ecuador, along with the Spanish conquerors of the Inka. Some Africans joined Indian groups and even took part in attacks on their former masters. Others, even enslaved Africans, won success on the battlefield and acquired their own estates and Indian slaves.

By the seventeenth century, Africans were everywhere in Spanish America. They were a major part of the mixed society that was taking shape in the Western Hemisphere as a result of the human Columbian Exchange. As you will see in the next chapter, Africans found allies and formed societies outside the limits set by their European masters.

THE FATE OF ESTEBAN

THE STORY OF A MAN GENERALLY KNOWN AS
Esteban shows how the Columbian Exchange
moved people and cultures around the globe. He
was born in Morocco, in North Africa, and spoke
Arabic. Most likely he was one of many people
from his region in the sixteenth century who fled
to Spain and accepted Christianity to escape
drought and civil war in their homelands. In
Spain he was bought as a slave by a Spaniard who
joined an expedition to the Americas led by an
ambitious duke named Pánfilo de Narváez. The
expedition consisted of more than four hundred
men. An unknown number of them were African.
One of these was Esteban.

The expedition landed in Florida in 1528. The
group hoped to find gold but instead met one
catastrophe after another. Narváez vanished at
sea. Indians, disease, accident, and starvation

picked off the rest, until only four were left. Esteban and his owner were two of them.

The little band headed west toward Mexico, eating spiders and ant eggs to survive, periodically enslaved, tortured, and humiliated by Indians. As they passed from one native realm to the next, the Indians came to believe that these wandering strangers had healing powers, and Esteban and the Spaniards encouraged this belief. Esteban was the scout who contacted each new culture as the group walked for thousands of miles across what is now the Southwest of the United States and into northern Mexico. In some ways he had become the leader of the group.

Eight years after leaving Spain, the four survivors of the Narváez expedition entered Mexico City. The three Spaniards were celebrated as heroes. Esteban was enslaved again and sold to a new owner, who sent him north with another expedition, this time to

search for mythical cities of gold.

Esteban never returned from that journey. According to the Spanish account, he was captured by Indians in the mountains on the Arizona–New Mexico border, and then killed when he tried to escape. The Zuni people of the region tell different stories. In one version told to me, the Indians welcomed Esteban. He was like no other man they had ever seen, and they believed his spirit held great knowledge. So they cut off his lower legs so he could never leave and kept him alive and honored, but unable to walk, for many years.

Esteban's true fate may never be known for sure. Along with many others, he was swept from one world to the next, like a cork on a current of water, by the swirling tides of the Columbian Exchange and the harsh realities of slavery.

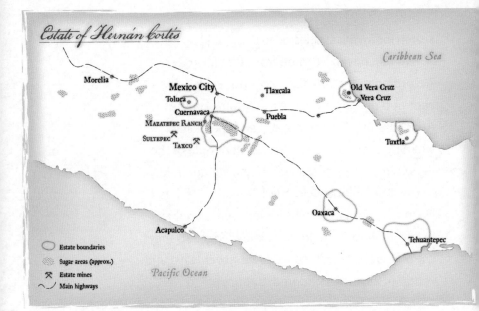

Estate of Hernán Cortés

Caribbean Sea

Morelia

Mexico City   Tlaxcala   Old Vera Cruz
Toluca   Vera Cruz
Cuernavaca
Mazatepec Ranch   Puebla
Sultepec
         Taxco   Tuxtla

                                              Oaxaca

Acapulco   Tehuantepec

⬭ Estate boundaries
▦ Sugar areas (approx.)
⚒ Estate mines
〰 Main highways   Pacific Ocean

A Hybrid Society

The intimate mingling of Europeans and Indians in the Americas began in 1493, at Columbus's ill-fated colony of La Isabela. Most of the Spaniards on the expedition were young, single men. A census from 1514 shows that only a third of them were married—and most were married to women of the Taino people. A few years later, Cortés, the conqueror of Mexico, fathered several children with native women. One of them was a daughter of Motecuhzoma, the famous "Montezuma" who was held captive by Cortés and killed in 1520 during the battle to drive the Spanish out of Mexico City.

Cortés did not hide his half-Indian, illegitimate children. In fact, he arranged a marriage for one of his daughters and ensured that his half-Indian son would be recognized as a full member of Spanish society, even including him in his will. (Cortés's oldest legitimate son and his half-Indian son battled in court for years over Cortés's estate—they fought over the ownership of Indian slaves.)

The Spanish Crown encouraged pairings between Spaniards and Indians, although they believed that such pairings should lead

(*left*)
Estate of Hernán
Cortés, 1547

to Christian marriages. Some elite Indians also saw that they could reinforce their status by marrying their daughters to Spaniards in Christian ceremonies. For many Spanish men, though, a Taino ceremony was more useful than a Christian one. By marrying a native woman, a low-ranking Spaniard could gain access to the goods and workers that the high-ranking Indians controlled.

A hybrid society came into existence, first in the Caribbean and then everywhere else in the Americas. The mixing began at the top, with the commanders of the conquistadors. Marrying into noble or elite families was a way for the conquerors to justify or reinforce their rule over the peoples they had conquered. The mixed-blood offspring of conquistadors such as Cortés and Francisco Pizarro, conqueror of the Inka Empire, became some of the most powerful citizens in the new colonies.

At first, few of the hybrid children had African blood. This changed as plantation slavery spread. The percentage of the total American population that was African rose, as did the number of Afro-Indians, Afro-Europeans, and Afro-Euro-Indians. By 1570 there were three times as many

(right)
Conquistadors often married into the ruling families of the peoples they conquered. In Mexico and Peru, Cortés and Pizarro and their generals fathered a generation of mixed-culture children who became some of the new colonies' most powerful citizens.

AMERICAN IMPERIAL FAMILIES OF THE 15TH AND 16TH CENTURY

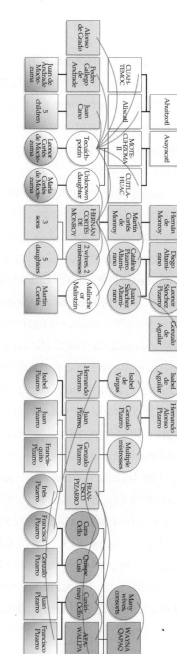

Legend:

Mexica (EMPEROR)

Spaniard (CONQUEROR)

Inka (EMPEROR)

Mixed Mexica-Spanish

Mixed Inka-Spanish

⟩ Spouse or mate

▭ | or | ▭ — Lineal descent

──── Full sibling (shared parents)

– – – Sibling (shared father, mother uncertain)

To bolster the legitimacy of their rule, conquistadors often married into or took consorts from the elite of the peoples they conquered. Cortés and Pizarro being among the leading examples. They created a generation of mixed-culture children who became some of the new colonies' most powerful citizens. Because many of the conquistadors were from Extremadura, a mountainous region dominated by a few interrelated families, they were often as tightly related as Indian nobility. The result was a multicultural family web unlike any other.

Africans as Europeans in Mexico and twice as many people of mixed parentage. Seventy years later there were still three times as many Africans as Europeans, but twenty-three times as many mixed people. Most of these were free Afro-Europeans.

Europeans of the sixteenth century did not have the same ideas about "race" as later generations. They did not see themselves as being different from Africans or Indians on a biological level. They did worry, however, about moral differences. Many Spaniards believed that people passed on to their children their own ideas and moral characters, and that these features were fixed and unchangeable. For example, a mother who was born Jewish or Muslim would somehow pass the essence of being Jewish or Muslim to her children, even if she never exposed them to the religion.

The Indians of the Americas were not seen at first as a threat of this sort. Unlike Muslims or Jews, who had supposedly rejected Christianity, Indians had never heard of Christ and so had not had the opportunity to reject the Gospel. Over time, though, it became clear that many Indians were resisting full Christianization. As a result,

(right)
The cultural and ethnic jumble in the streets of Spain's American colonies was often reflected in art. This eighteenth-century painting shows the Virgin Mary embedded in the great silver mountain of Potosí, uniting Christianity with the Andean tradition that mountains embody the gods.

Europeans became suspicious of the whole class of Indians. By the second half of the sixteenth century, European elites in Spanish America started to fear that mixed-blood relationships were leading to a kind of moral contamination of the colonists' bloodlines. The earlier, freewheeling attitude toward mixed-blood relationships and people became stricter.

Spanish governments started passing laws that limited the rights of mixed people in the colonies, such as forbidding them to carry weapons, become priests, or practice certain trades. Dozens of new rules targeted Africans and Indians as well as mixed people. Men and women with African blood, for example, could not be seen in the streets after 8:00 p.m., and they could not gather in groups of more than four in public places. Women of mixed native and European blood could not wear Indian clothing. Afro-European women could not wear Spanish-style jewelry. A Spanish butcher who cheated his customers received a fine. An Indian butcher who did the same thing received a hundred lashes with a whip.

As the restrictions increased, so did colonists' fear of the people they were restricting. Some worried that Africans and Indians were secretly plotting to attack Christians. An elaborate system called *casta* arose to classify people by their moral and spiritual worth, based on their descent. Each group was thought to have a basic, unchanging moral nature. A mulatto (Afro-European) was different from a mestizo (Indo-European), and both were different from a zambo (Afro-Indian). The children of various combinations also had their own labels, such as coyote, wolf, white-spotted, or suspended-in-air.

The *casta* system did not work quite as the government intended. Instead of being confined to their social slots, people used the categories as tools to better their conditions. They searched for the identity that best suited them. For example, when one half-Indian son of a conquistador married a native noblewoman, their son should have been classified as a coyote in the *casta* system. Instead he was declared to be an Indian and became a governor. Meanwhile, other Indians claimed to be Africans, because slaves paid fewer taxes, and the Indians didn't see why they should pay them, either. Local officials who were supposed to police the *casta* categories were short of cash, so they sold people whatever identities they wanted.

Casta paintings were intended to instruct outsiders about the cultural mixes in Spain's American colonies. (*Left top*) Spaniard and Negro Makes Mulatto; (*Left bottom*) Negro and Indian Makes Wolf; (*Right top*) Chamizo and Indian Makes Cambuja; (*Right bottom*) Spaniard and Albino Makes Return-Backwards.

13.
De Chamizo é india
sale Cambuja. Chamizo 1.
india 2. Cambuja 3.

The laws against Indian slavery made things even more complicated. Under Spanish law, children inherited the status of their mothers. In theory, this meant that the children of Indian women could not be enslaved, no matter who their father was. African men sought out non-African spouses so that their children would not become slaves. Colonial authorities tried to enslave Afro-European and Afro-Indian children anyway, but many of them simply moved away and told their new neighbors that they were Spaniards or Indians.

The population of Mexico became increasingly blended over time. By the end of the eighteenth century, "pure" Africans were disappearing. Disease and intermarriage were reducing the number of "pure" Indians at a rapid rate. Even the remaining "pure" Spaniards (a tiny group that in Mexico City made up only 5 percent of the population) were marrying outside their category so fast that soon they would no longer exist. Yet even as it became more difficult to see the differences among people, colonial authorities tried ever harder to keep them separate.

Anxiety over ethnic and racial identity is

reflected in a special kind of art produced in Spain's American colonies: *casta* paintings. These sets of images, usually sixteen to a set, illustrate the different categories of people recognized by the casta system. Each image is labeled: "From Black Man and Indian Woman, Wolf" or "From Mulatto Man and Mestiza Woman, Wolf-Suspended-in-Air." For all their care to show the *casta* categories, however, the paintings fail to show one group that was present in Spanish America.

JOHNNY GOOD-LOOKING

SOMETIME AFTER 1500 A YOUNG WEST AFRICAN
man arrived in Portugal, possibly as a slave,
possibly as a representative of a family that
wanted to sell slaves to Europeans. Either way, he
changed course and crossed the border into Spain.
A hint of his personality comes through in the
Spanish name he chose for himself: Juan Garrido,
which means, roughly, Johnny Good-Looking.

Garrido crossed the Atlantic early in the
sixteenth century as a conquistador. He
accompanied the Spanish takeover of the island
of Puerto Rico and Ponce de Léon's useless
quest for the Fountain of Youth. When Cortés
conquered the Triple Alliance (as the Aztec

Empire of Mexico was known), Garrido was at his side. Afterward, at the request of Cortés, Garrido built a chapel to the memory of Spaniards who had been sacrificed in bloody Aztec rituals. Garrido's biggest contribution, though, came after Cortés found three grains of wheat in a sack of rice. The conqueror asked Garrido to plant them in a plot next to the chapel.

Not only were the Spanish eager for wheat from which they could make beer and bread, but the church needed bread in order to celebrate Mass properly. All earlier attempts to grow wheat in Hispaniola had failed in the island's hot, humid climate. Two of Garrido's grains, however, sprouted. From them came more grains, and, as a Spanish historian wrote in 1552, "little by little there was boundless wheat."

Garrido's wheat was greeted with joy. In a strange land, it was a taste of home. Soon golden wheat waved in the breeze across central Mexico,

An African man, possibly Juan Garrido, holds Hernán Cortés's horse as the conquistador approaches Motecuhzoma, leader of the Triple Alliance.

replacing corn and forest. Garrido's wheat may even have traveled north into Texas and up the Mississippi. If this is true, much of the wheat that turned the American Midwest into an agricultural powerhouse in the nineteenth century came from an African conquistador's roadside chapel in Mexico City.

In planting the wheat, Garrido helped make the Columbian Exchange happen. At the same time, he was part of the exchange, as were Cortés and the other foreigners. Garrido lived with his family in the center of busy, crowded, multiethnic and multicultural Mexico City. An African turned European turned American, he is a symbol of that city of exiles and travelers.

No trace of Garrido's life after 1538 has been found. He probably died in the next decade, forgotten in the hubbub and tumult of the New World he had helped to create.

Asians in New Spain

Asians came to the Americas, too.
They came by means of the galleon trade
that carried silver across the Pacific to Asia
and Chinese goods back across the Pacific to
Mexico, as described in chapter 5. One historian
estimates that fifty to a hundred thousand
Asians arrived in Spanish America as servants,
slaves, or sailors who worked on the long
Pacific voyages that set sail from Manila in
the Philippines. As many as 60 to 80 percent
of the galleons' crews may have been Asian.
Many never went back to Manila. Over the
decades, thousands of sailors jumped ship in the
Americas, taking jobs in shipyards or building
forts and other public works.

Sometimes Asian sailors worked alongside
Asian slaves from India, Malaysia, Borneo, and
other countries of Southeast Asia. Although
Manila banned Asian slavery in 1672, the ban
was not very effective. Almost a century later,
Mexican authorities forced a religious group
from Manila to get rid of twenty Asian servants
who were being treated too much like slaves.

Known by the Spaniards as *chinos*, Asian
migrants spread slowly throughout Mexico.

Among them were Japanese samurai who had been stranded outside their homeland when Japan closed its borders in the 1630s. The Spanish authorities allowed the samurai to use their traditional weapons to protect silver shipments along the highway from Mexico City to the ports. The results were so encouraging that the authorities began drafting mixed-race people into the militias. By the eighteenth century, Afro-Indo-Asian units were protecting mail deliveries, patrolling for bandits, and driving off attacking British ships. When the British admiral-pirate George Anson invaded western Mexico in 1741, the multicultural force played a major role in his defeat.

The Mexican city of Puebla had a tight-knit Asian community. Its members may have contributed to one of the city's most important industries: ceramics, especially fake Chinese pottery. The Asian community in Mexico City was larger. The first real Chinatown in the Americas, it was centered on an outdoor Asian marketplace in a big plaza in the middle of town. Chinese tailors, shoemakers, butchers, musicians, and goldsmiths competed with African, Indian, and Spanish shopkeepers for business.

(*right*)
A Japanese samurai in armor, shown in an eighteenth-century watercolor.

In the 1630s, a rivalry developed between Spanish barbers and Chinese barbers. In those days a barber did not just cut hair but also performed dental surgery. The Chinese barbers had an advantage, because Chinese dentistry was the most advanced in the world. Wealthy customers flocked to their stands. At the urging of Spanish barbers, the city council tried several times to ban Chinese barbers from the city center, but the bans failed—perhaps because influential customers did not want to travel far to have their hair cut and their teeth cleaned.

The First Global City

Mexico City in the sixteenth century
was a giddy buzz and snarl of African slaves,
Asian shopkeepers, Indian farmers and laborers,
and European priests, soldiers, and second-level
aristocrats. Its multitude of ethnic groups from
Africa, Asia, Europe, and the Americas made it the
world's first truly global city. It was the place where
East met West under an African and Indian gaze.
Its inhabitants were ashamed of the genetic mix yet
proud of their city's worldly culture. In *Grandeza
Mexicana*, a two-hundred-page love letter to his home,
poet Bernardo de Balbuena wrote of Mexico City:

(*left*)
Carried across the Pacific from Manila by the galleon trade, the Chinese artist Esteban Sampzon became one of Buenos Aires's leading sculptors at the end of the eighteenth century. *His Christ of Humility and Patience* (ca. 1790) still adorns the city's Basílica de Nuestra Señora de la Merced.

Spain is joined with China, Italy with Japan, and finally an entire world in trade and order.

Think of Mexico City as the first twenty-first-century city, the forerunner to today's modern, globalized megacities. It may seem foolish to use terms such as modern and globalized to describe a city with no mass communication, or a time when shipping goods from one place to the next took months or years. Even today, though, billions of people on our networked planet have no telephones. Even today the reach of goods and services from high-technology places such as Japan, Europe, and the United States is limited. Modernity is a patchy thing, a matter of shifting light and dark upon the globe. Mexico City was one of the spots it touched first.

northeastern coast of Brazil, was a slave port
that became the first glimpse of the Americas
for more than 1.5 million captive Africans. The
slaves were supposed to spend the rest of their
days in Brazil's sugar plantations and mills.
Most did, but thousands escaped their bondage.
Many of these created fugitive communities
in the nation's forests—"inventing liberty," in
the words of Brazilian historian João José Reis.
Almost always they were joined by Indians, who
were also targeted by European slavers.

These illegal settlements have been called by
many names: *quilombos*, *mocambos*, *palenques*,
and *cumbes*. In English they are usually called
"maroon" communities, from *símaran*, which
means "flight of an arrow" in the language of
the Taino people. During the era of slavery,
thousands of these communities dotted Brazil,

the rest of South America, most of the Caribbean
and Central America, and even parts of North
America. More than fifty existed in what is now
the United States.

Protected by steep hillsides, dense forest,
treacherous rivers, and lethal booby traps, these
illegal hybrid settlements endured for decades,
even centuries. Most were small, but some
grew to amazing sizes. The *quilombo* Liberdade
(Liberty), in northeastern Brazil, now has a
population of six hundred thousand. It is said
to be the largest Afro-American community in
the Western Hemisphere. These societies are a
part of American history that has not often been
recognized.

A New View of the Great Encounter

Columbus's voyage began a great encounter
between two halves of the world. It was less a
meeting of Europe and the American wilderness
than of Africans and Indians. The relationships
between the captive Africans and the Indians
were forged in the cage of slavery and in the
uprisings against it. Largely conducted out
of sight of Europeans, the complex interplay
between Indians and Africans is a hidden

QUILOMBO CAMPINHO DA INDEPENDENCIA
8 ANOS DE TITULAÇAO
21-03-1999
21-03-2005
Valorize
...Tem historia
SEJA BEM

history that researchers are only now beginning to unearth.

Even when schoolbooks recognize that the majority of people in the American colonies were Africans and Indians, those groups are often shown as helpless victims. Indians melt away before the onslaught of white colonists. Africans are chained on plantations, working under the lash. They have little will of their own and little control over their lives.

Slavery did force millions of Africans and Indians into lives of misery and pain. Often those lives were short. A third to half of the slaves in Brazil died within four or five years. More still died on the journey inside Africa to the slave ports, or on the passage across the Atlantic. Yet people always seek ways to act on their will, even in the most terrible circumstances. Africans and Indians in the American colonies were no different. They fought with each other, borrowed each other's identities, and formed alliances for common goals. In all cases, though, their goal was always the same: freedom.

They won freedom more often than most people realize. Slaves vanished from their

(right)
Boys in a *quilombo* in the Amazon Basin, 2012.

masters' control by the tens or even hundreds of thousands in Brazil, Peru, and the Caribbean. Spain recognized self-governing maroon communities in its colonies Ecuador, Colombia, Panama, and Mexico. In Suriname, in northeastern South America, so-called Bush Negroes fought a century-long war with the proud Dutch government and, in 1762, pushed it into a humiliating peace treaty. In Florida, a maroon-Indian alliance fought two wars with the U.S. government and succeeded in winning liberty for its population of escaped slaves—the only time before the Emancipation Proclamation (issued during the U.S. Civil War) that the government freed a class of slaves. Most important, slaves in Haiti, on the Caribbean island of Hispaniola, created an entire maroon nation by driving out the French in an 1804 revolution that terrified slave owners across Europe and the Americas.

Africans in Charge

One of the most lasting myths about the slave trade is that all Africans were helpless pawns. In fact, Africans themselves controlled the supply of African slaves. They sold slaves to Europeans in the numbers they chose and at prices they negotiated as equals.

If Africans were not forced by Europeans to sell other Africans, why did they do it? The beliefs, attitudes, and values of the past were not the same as those of the present. Few Europeans or Africans of the sixteenth and seventeenth centuries saw slavery as something that needed to be explained, or as an evil to be condemned. Slavery was part of the furniture of everyday life. In both Europe and Africa, depriving others of their liberty wasn't wrong in and of itself—although it was bad to enslave the wrong person. Christians were not generally supposed to enslave fellow Christians, for example. Africans sold other Africans into slavery more often than Europeans did, but this had less to do with ideas about liberty than with different economic systems.

In western and central Europe, the most important form of property was land. The aristocracy consisted mostly of large landowners who could buy or sell property. In western and central Africa, however, land was owned by the government—sometimes personally by the king, sometimes by a family or religious group, but usually by the state itself. Land could not readily be taxed or sold. What could be taxed and sold was labor. Under African law, slaves were the only recognized kind of private, income-producing property.

As in the case of white Europeans, Africans could be sentenced to slavery for committing a crime or to repay a debt. The most common way to acquire slaves in Africa, though, was by war. Captives would be taken by a king or given to middlemen, who would sell them to customers in North Africa or Europe. Slaves in Africa might be granted liberty after a period of service, either because they were related to their owners or because they were still useful to the monarch as subjects. In addition, some slaves in Africa did not have to work hard or for long periods of time. Wealthy, powerful slave owners often kept more slaves than they needed, just as rich European landowners would pile up unused land, because slaves were a sign of wealth and status.

At the beginning of the Atlantic slave trade, when European ships first became a constant presence on African shores, the two economic systems did not seem that different. After all, Europeans could buy and sell labor—that was the purpose of indentured servitude—and

Africans could "own" land by controlling the labor of the people who used that land. The key difference was that labor is portable and land is not. Laborers, in other words, could be moved from place to place.

When Europeans arrived in Africa, they easily tapped into the existing slave trade. African governments and merchants who were already shipping human beings could increase production to satisfy the foreigners' demands. African demand was as important as European demand in the growth of the slave trade. African merchants bought slaves from African armies, raiders, and pirates and paid African guards to take them to African-run holding tanks. Once a sale was arranged, Africans loaded the captives onto European-owned slave ships—which often had Africans among their crews. Other Africans supplied the ships with goods such as food, rope, water, and timber for the voyage across the Atlantic.

Yet an enormous change was taking place in the age-old institution of slavery. Before the Atlantic slave trade, most African slaveholders knew something about their slaves' previous lives. The chattel slavery in the American colonies made slaves anonymous. Slaveholders generally

knew and cared nothing about their slaves' lives. Often they didn't even see their human property—many slaveholders lived far away, safe from disease in European cities. No longer were slaves an owner's relatives or vanquished enemies. They were units of labor, to be disposed of based only on their economic value.

Because European slave dealers and owners had little knowledge of the origins of the unhappy men and women on their ships or in their fields, they did not realize that many of the captive Africans were prisoners of war, people with military backgrounds who could organize escapes and rebellions. In their hunger for labor, European sugar growers were importing people who would have liked nothing better than to destroy them—people such as Aqualtune, founder of Palmares.

Rebels, Runaways, and Secret Cities

Back in Africa, the story goes, Aqualtune was a princess and a general. She is said to have ruled a state in what is now central Angola. Around 1605 she was captured in battle, sold to Portuguese slavers, and shipped to the Americas. She landed at the sugar port of Recife,

(left)
From the summit of Serra da Barriga, the maroons of Palmares could see every movement below.

at the tip of Brazil's "bulge" into the Atlantic.

A military strategist, Aqualtune naturally began to plan her escape. Within months she was in the backcountry with about forty followers. On the peak of a tall hill twenty-five miles from the coast, home to a community of native people, she founded Palmares. Today that peak is a national park, with a plaque telling Aqualtune's story— although nobody knows how much of it is true.

What is known is that thirty thousand or more Africans fled to that hill and other nearby peaks in the 1620s and 1630s, taking advantage of the confusion when Dutch forces attacked and occupied the sugar towns of the Brazilian coast. Free of European control, the escapees built up as many as twenty tight-knit settlements centered on Palmares. These were havens for African, native, and European runaways. At its height in the 1650s, the maroon state of Palmares ruled an area of more than ten thousand square miles and had nearly as many inhabitants as the English colonies in North America. It was as if a small African nation had been scooped up and planted in the Americas.

The capital of Palmares was called Macaco, located in the place where modern legend says

(right)
European societies always showed their conflicts with maroons as victories. In the Battle of Okeechobee, fought on Christmas Day, 1837, US forces were driven back with twice as many dead and more wounded than the Seminoles. Yet this 1878 engraving shows the Seminoles melting away before the soldiers' heroic, bayonet-wielding charge.

Aqualtune came to rest beside a natural spring of clear water after her escape. Spread along a wide street were a church, a council house, four small ironworks, and several hundred homes. Irrigated fields surrounded the settlement. The head of state in the 1650s was Aqualtune's son, Ganga Zumba, who lived in what one European visitor described as a "palace." Ganga Zumba was treated like a king. His subjects had to approach him on their knees, clapping their hands in an African gesture of respect and obedience.

Palmares was led by Africans from Angola, but it was a mixed society. Many of its people were Indians. Some were Europeans with uneasy relations to their own societies, including Jews, suspected witches, and escaped criminals. Most of Palmares's people looked like Africans, but they lived in Indian-style homes. Their religious ceremonies seem to have been a mix of Christian, African, and Indian elements. Their political organization, though, was African, with Aqualtune's children and grandchildren in charge.

Knowing that his people were always at risk of attack, Ganga Zumba organized the towns more like military camps than farming villages, with strict discipline and constant guard duty.

Each major settlement was ringed by a double
wooden wall with watchtowers at the corners.
These walls were protected by snarls of timber,
hidden pits lined with poisonous stakes, and
fields of caltrops (three or more iron spikes
welded together so that one spike always pointed
up, ready to injure anyone who stepped on it).
Every single person who fled slavery to live in
Palmares had risked life and limb for liberty.
Palmares bristled with their determination to
keep command over their own destiny.

Maroons in Hispaniola had eventually driven
the sugar industry away from the island, to
mainland Mexico. Portuguese officials now feared
that Palmares would do the same thing in Brazil.
The rebels were a direct challenge to the colony.
Not only did troops from Palmares raid Portuguese
settlements, but the location of Palmares blocked
further European movement into that part of the
Brazilian interior. Between 1643 and 1677 the
Portuguese sent troops to attack Palmares more
than twenty times, always unsuccessfully. Finally,
in 1694, a determined assault overcame the
defenses of Macaco. Its fall, however, was anything
but the end of *quilombos* and maroons in Brazil or
anywhere else in the Americas.

THE RISE AND FALL OF ZUMBI

ZUMBI WAS A NEPHEW OF GANGA ZUMBA
who became military commander of Palmares.
Captured as an infant by Europeans, he was
raised by a priest in a coastal town. In 1670, as
a teenager, he ran back to Palmares, although
he returned to the priest for sentimental visits.
Zumbi was well educated and knowledgeable
about the Europeans. He rose quickly to
command the forces of Palmares.

In 1678, Ganga Zumba, weary of war, made
a peace treaty with the Portuguese, who had
captured some of his children and grandchildren
and were holding them hostage. Zumbi saw this
treaty as a sellout of everything the maroons
stood for. Angered beyond measure, he poisoned

his uncle the king, seized the throne, and tore up the treaty. The war was on again.

Appalled by the meager results of the forty-year campaign against Palmares, the Portugese governor-general decided to try something new. He made a deal with a *bandeirante*, or backwoodsman, named Domingos Jorge Velho. The governor promised supplies, loot, a bounty for every captured African, and full pardons for previous crimes if Jorge Velho used his private army to bring down Palmares.

After a five-hundred-mile march, the *bandeirantes* attacked Macaco, scrambling up the hill through a maze of defenses with maroons firing down at them from the walls. Jorge Velho then told his men to build sturdy, movable

wooden barricades. Crouching behind these, his men shoved and wedged the barricades up the hill a few feet at a time as arrows and bullets thunked into the other side of the wood.

Zumbi paced the walls of Macaco, rallying his exhausted forces. He saw that *bandeirantes* had killed two maroon sentries and were within a few feet of the walls. Some of his own men tore down part of a wall to attack the *bandeirantes*, and the invaders poured into Macaco. Hundreds died in the bloody, confused nighttime battle, but Zumbi escaped the fall of Macaco. He continued to skirmish with the Portuguese for more than a year, until one of his followers betrayed his location. Zumbi was ambushed and killed in 1695. All along the coast, colonists celebrated the victory, parading through the streets with torches night after night in a festival of joy.

(*right*)
Portuguese Expansion into Brazil

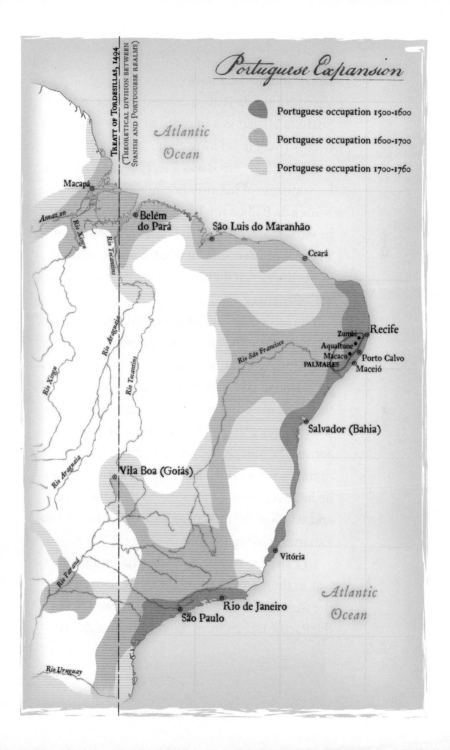

TREATY OF TORDESILLAS, 1494
(THEORETICAL DIVISION BETWEEN
SPANISH AND PORTUGUESE REALMS)

Atlantic
Ocean

Portuguese occupation 1500-1600

Portuguese occupation 1600-1700

Portuguese occupation 1700-1760

Macapá

Amazon

Rio Xingu

Rio Tocantins

Belém
do Pará

São Luis do Maranhão

Ceará

Rio Xingu

Rio Araguaia

Rio Tocantins

Rio São Francisco

Zumbi   Recife
Aqualtune
Macaco   Porto Calvo
PALMARES
Maceió

Salvador (Bahia)

Rio Araguaia

Vila Boa (Goiás)

Rio Paraná

Vitória

Atlantic
Ocean

Rio de Janeiro

São Paulo

Rio Uruguay

Drake and the Maroons

Vasco Núñez de Balboa crossed the ocean from Spain to Hispaniola in 1500, when he was about twenty-five. He set himself up as a farmer in a remote village, but it was a terrible career choice for someone of his ambition and reckless spirit. Núñez de Balboa ran up debts. To escape them, he stowed away in a barrel on a ship bound for a new Spanish colony in what is now Colombia, in northwestern South America, near the border with Panama.

The settlement in Colombia had been established to find gold mines. Labor would come from enslaving the local Indians. The Indians saw no reason to take part in this scheme and showed their lack of enthusiasm by riddling the invaders with poisoned arrows. Once Núñez de Balboa arrived, he quickly became one of the Spanish captain's most valued lieutenants. Within a year he had overthrown the captain, taken his place, and set off at the head of an expedition north into Panama, looking for gold.

In Panama, Núñez de Balboa hacked his way to the top of a mountain range, looked to the west, and became the first European to see the Pacific Ocean from the American side. Yet

he and his men were stunned to discover that
an entire community of escaped African slaves
was living in those mountains. (It is likely, in
fact, that an African saw the Pacific Ocean from
the American side before a European did.) The
discovery also meant that the region was a good
place for escaped slaves to avoid capture.

Núñez de Balboa was executed in 1519 for
his shenanigans, but his sighting of the Pacific
had electrified the Spanish. Before long, Spain
founded two colonies on the isthmus, or narrow
strip of land, that separates the Atlantic and
Pacific Oceans. Panama was on the Pacific coast
and Nombre de Dios was on the Atlantic. The
idea was that spices from an island group in
Asia, which Spain intended to capture, would be
shipped to Panama, carried on a new road across
the isthmus, and sent from Nombre de Dios to
Spain. When Spain failed to capture the Spice
Islands, though, both would-be ports shrank.
Then, in 1545, silver was discovered at Potosí, in
Bolivia, as described in chapter 5. Half or more
of the silver from this rich strike was shipped up
the Pacific coast of South America to the colony
of Panama. Instead of spices, it was silver that
was carried across the isthmus to Nombre de

Dios to be shipped to Spain.

The road across the isthmus became a critical chokepoint for the Spanish Empire. Down that single passage flowed much of the monarchy's financial lifeblood. Maintaining the road through jungles and over mountains took a lot of work, as did hauling the king's silver across the isthmus. The colonists first used Indian slaves imported from other colonies. After the Spanish monarchy banned Indian slavery, the colonists turned to Africa.

By 1565, Africans outnumbered Europeans in the isthmus seven to one. Unsurprisingly, the Europeans found it hard to control their human property. Runaways grouped by the hundreds into multiethnic villages that were joined by Indians. United by their loathing of Spaniards, the maroons liberated slaves, killed colonists, and stole mules and cattle.

The maroon problem was noticed as early as 1521. By the 1550s the number of maroons in the isthmus was estimated at twelve hundred. Their leader was a man whose name is sometimes given as Bayano. Like Aqualtune, he seems to have been a captured military leader. He oversaw the building of a walled fortress on a hill outside

(right)
In the centuries of the slave trade, escaped Africans and their descendants scattered across the hemisphere and mixed with native groups. Many formed microstates whose tenacious struggle for liberty created large free areas in the Americas long before the United States existed.

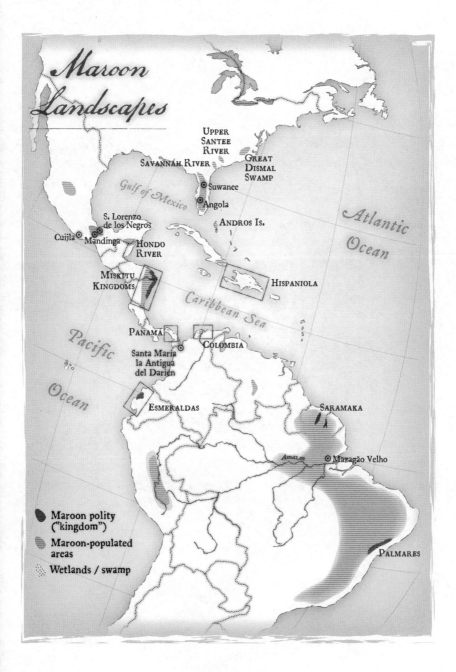

Maroon
Landscapes

UPPER
SANTEE
RIVER

SAVANNAH RIVER

GREAT
DISMAL
SWAMP

Gulf of Mexico

⊙ Suwanee

⊙ Angola

ANDROS IS.

S. Lorenzo
de los Negros

Cuijla ⊙

Mandinga

HONDO
RIVER

HISPANIOLA

MISKITU
KINGDOMS

Caribbean Sea

Atlantic
Ocean

Pacific

Ocean

PANAMA

COLOMBIA

Santa María
la Antigua
del Darién ⊙

ESMERALDAS

SARAMAKA

Amazon

⊙ Mazagão Velho

PALMARES

● Maroon polity
   ("kingdom")

● Maroon-populated
   areas

░ Wetlands / swamp

Nombre de Dios. Bayano's miniature kingdom was an ethnic mix: Indians from every region between Peru and Nicaragua, and a dozen different African ethnic groups.

Bayano was eventually captured by a deceitful Spaniard, but the maroon problem did not go away. Other communities sprang up. Spain realized that only a large-scale military campaign could solve the problem, but no one could agree on who should pay for this campaign, so nothing happened. Matters worsened for Spain when the maroons joined forces with the man who would become Spain's most hated enemy: Sir Francis Drake, the English pirate-privateer. On several occasions Drake plotted with a maroon leader to attack Spanish settlements. Their final plan was to ambush a one-hundred-twenty-mule silver convoy as it came down through the hills outside Nombre de Dios.

The ambush succeeded. Giddy but too weary to lug all the silver through the hills, Drake and his allies buried all but a few silver bars at the bottom of a nearby stream. Unfortunately for the pirates and the maroons, Spanish troops captured a French member of their group, discovered the location of the buried booty, and

(left)
Constantly hunted by slavers, the people of Brazil's *quilombos* sought spiritual comfort—and found it in religious observances that mixed African, Indian, and Christian elements. These limbs are votive offerings given as thanks for miraculous cures in a church considered holy to both Catholicism and the Afro-Indian religion Candomblé.

Seringa *(Hevea brasiliensis)* rubber, bird attractant, fish food

Açaí *(Euterpe oleracea)*: fruit, heart of palm, timber

Andiroba *(Carapa guianensis)*: lamp oil, bug repellent, medicines

Lemon *(Citrus limon)*: fruit

Acasuzeira: timber (poles, firewood)

Aninga *(Montrichardia linifera)*: Erosion control, fish/shrimp habitat

Inga *(Inga edulis)* fruit bird and monkey attractant

Pão Mulato
(Mirtaceoe facies)
timber (needs fire,
light to grow, so
disturbance indicator)

Acasuzeira:
timber (poles,
firewood)

Seringa *(Hevea
brasiliensis)*
rubber—many
uses

ango *(Mangifera
op.)* fruit (intro.
om India)

Açaí *(Euterpe
oleracea)*
see above

Guava *(Psidium
spp.)*: fruit, fish
food

The riverbank across
from Maria do
Rosario's home may
look like a tropical
hodgepodge, but al-
most every plant was
sown and tended
by Rosario and her
family, creating an
environment both
ecologically rich and
artificial.

recovered nearly all the silver before Drake's men returned for it. The episode failed to enrich Drake, but the attacks on Spanish settlements were a triumph for the maroons.

Afro-Indian States

Reports that the maroons in Panama had allied themselves with pirates horrified the Spanish Crown. Colonial officials demanded that the king send a fleet to clean out the maroons. While the court dragged its feet, maroons continued to steal cattle, free slaves, and kill Spaniards. Meanwhile, English, French, and Dutch pirates showed up on the isthmus and asked the maroons to help them against the Spanish as they had helped Drake. Most got no help—the maroons seem to have formed a low opinion of Europeans.

Fears of a pirate-maroon alliance continued to grow, especially in 1578–1579, when Drake sailed up the Pacific coast of South America, wrecking Spanish possessions along the way. Colonial officials made deals with Domingo Congo, head of the maroons in Bayano's old territory, and other maroon leaders. In exchange for farmland, livestock, and (most important) liberty, the

(right)
Hundreds of *quilombos* formed in the lower Amazon, where rivers spill over their banks twice a day at high tide. Rivers are the main transport routes, so villages spread out along the banks. Houses are built on stilts to let the tidewater pass beneath the floorboards.

maroons agreed to be loyal to the king. The agreements did not stop future escapes. Runaways continued to disappear into the forest until the end of the slave trade. By that time, though, maroons had won the highest kind of liberty. They were ordinary citizens.

Governments throughout the Americas wiped out many maroon groups, but others won their freedom. In Mexico, escaped African slaves negotiated with colonial authorities to win legal freedom for three African towns. In Central America the kingdom of Miskitu, populated by African and Indian refugees, controlled its own destiny for more than three centuries, until the modern nation of Nicaragua absorbed it in 1894.

In the United States, maroon communities of Indians and Africans formed in hard-to-reach places such as the Great Dismal Swamp of Virginia and North Carolina. In Florida, which was claimed by Spain until 1763, Spanish authorities established a town for escaped slaves from the English colonies who agreed to be loyal to Spain. Founded in 1739, Gracia Real de Santa Teresa de Mosé was the first legally recognized free African-American community north of Mexico.

Most maroons in Florida, however, went deep into the interior, into the territory of the Seminole tribe. The Seminole and the African maroons formed a strong alliance that fell apart only after 1821, when the United States acquired Florida. The Seminole were determined to resist all efforts to move them from their homeland to a reservation in Oklahoma. In 1839, a U.S. army commander, weary of fighting the Seminole, came up with a winning strategy to divide the Indian and African allies. He promised that any Africans who gave up fighting and agreed to settle in the West would be given their freedom. Slowly this offer broke up the Seminole-maroon alliance. Its success is understandable. It gave the maroons something for which they had been fighting for a century and a half: liberty.

Microstates of escaped Africans, Indians, and their descendants once existed across large areas of the Americas. Long before the American Revolution, these communities fought for liberty, and some of them won.

The Struggle Continues
In 1991, Maria do Rosario Costa Cabral and her siblings bought twenty-five acres of

land in Brazil's northeasternmost province. Dona Rosario had been born into a maroon community that was so poor, she told me, that her family cut matches in half lengthwise to make a box of matches last longer. Her father spent his days as a rubber tapper. Anytime he and his friends found an especially productive group of trees, or started farming a few acres of an abandoned plantation, wealthier people would show up with guns, call them squatters with no right to the trees or land, and push them out.

Little changed when Dona Rosario reached adulthood. Repeatedly she set up farms, and repeatedly she was pushed off them. Still, she jumped at the opportunity to buy land, even though the acres she and her family purchased had been ravaged in the 1980s by the overharvesting of palm trees. "The land was looted," she says. "It was a mass of vines and scrub."

She set out to bring it back with techniques she had learned from her father. With help from her sisters and brothers, she planted fast-growing timber trees for the sawmills upriver. For the market, they put in fruit trees. With woven shrimp traps like those used in West

Africa, they caught shrimp and kept them alive in cages that drifted in the creek. At the river's edge they planted trees that would produce seeds and fruit to attract fish. To an outsider, the result looked like a wild tropical landscape, but almost every species in it had been chosen and tended by Dona Rosario and her family.

The property was on the edge of a sprawling *quilombo* that had been in existence since 1770. After Brazil abolished slavery in 1888, the people of Brazil's *quilombos* did not have to fear a return to enslavement. Yet the end of slavery did not mean an end to discrimination, poverty, or antimaroon violence. The nation's maroon communities continued to conceal themselves. They stayed so far out of sight that by the middle of the twentieth century, most Brazilians believed *quilombos* no longer existed.

In the 1960s, the generals who then ruled Brazil looked at their maps and saw, to their displeasure, that about 60 percent of the country was blank. Actually, it was filled with Indians, peasant farmers, and *quilombos*, but the government paid no attention to these. Filling the blank spaces seemed to be a matter of national security. In a breathtakingly ambitious program, they linked the western frontier, the new capital city of Brasilia, and the ports of the Amazon River by slashing a network of highways across the interior.

In the 1970s and 1980s hundreds of thousands of migrants from central and southern Brazil thronged up the new highways. The generals had promised that they could begin new lives in new agricultural settlements. Instead they found bad roads, poor land, and lawless violence. Big ranches, many of which received financial aid from the government, viewed all people found on their property as squatters and removed them, often at gunpoint. Countless *quilombos* were wiped out, their inhabitants scattered. Then, in 1988, Brazil adopted a new, democratic constitution. One of its provisions was that *"quilombo* communities" were the legal owners of the land they occupied.

The drafters of the constitution thought that a few *quilombos* remained in the forest. Now researchers believe that as many as five thousand *quilombos* survive in Brazil, most of them in the Amazon Basin. Together they occupy perhaps one hundred fifteen thousand square miles, an

(right)
Vendors in the market of Belém, at the mouth of the Amazon, sell tree seeds for the region's farmers. Many farmers replant the forest with useful tree species like açai (celebrated for its fruit juice), bacuri (a fruit somewhat like a sweet-and-sour papaya), and bacaba (another popular fruit).

area the size of Italy, much of it desirable land along riverbanks. The people of these *quilombos* are now dealing with a rapid flood of change, some of it welcome, some of it not. Newcomers in the *quilombo* Mazagão Velho, for example, wanted to turn a traditional festival into a tourist attraction. They were replacing old costumes and masks with new ones. For more than two centuries the maroons in Mazagão Velho had been left largely alone. Now the world was coming in and, in the eyes of some residents, wrecking something they held dear.

Dona Rosario had entirely different feelings about coming out of the shadows. A new electric power line along the river meant that she could operate a cell phone charger. If someone in her family were hurt or sick, she could call for help. She was also able to buy an electric freezer, which meant she could store her açai berries while she called around to find the best price, rather than having to sell them for whatever she could get before they spoiled. For people who have always lived just a phone call away from an ambulance or police car, or who are used to frozen foods, this change is hard to grasp.

In January 2009, Dona Rosario stumbled

across a surveying party on her farm. Surveyors were planting stakes and tying ribbons, slicing up her holding into smaller parcels to sell. "I had a fit," she told me. "I said, 'I own this land, I planted this land.'" The surveyors ignored her.

Dona Rosario had grown up seeing her parents lose one piece of land after the next. Now it was happening to her. One difference between her and her parents, though, was that she had a phone. Another was that she had some things of value: a freezer full of açai berries and a bank account. She called government inspectors and showed her property documents to them, all the while threatening to hire a lawyer. The inspectors supported her claim to the land. The surveyors backed down.

Similar stories are being repeated throughout the Amazon region. Six months after Dona Rosario saw the surveyors off her land, Brazil passed Provisional Law 458, an ambitious attempt to sort out the tangled question of land ownership in Amazonia. The law granted land titles to maroon communities whose members occupied the land and had fewer than two hundred acres each. Industrial and environmental groups immediately challenged the law in court. They argued that the law would reward squatters for taking land illegally. Their alarm was easy to understand. The law would give control of a big part of the Amazon to its residents, and nobody was sure what they would do with it.

I happened to visit Dona Rosario not long after the president of Brazil signed Provisional Law 458. In her isolated area, she had heard little about the new law, but she nodded in forceful agreement when told about it. Her ancestors had come from Africa and blended with American natives to create something new. In their mixed way, they had taken care of the forest. It was no accident, she believed, that all the most valuable and beautiful parts of the Amazon were full of *quilombos*.

Forest may be the wrong word. Outsiders saw the region as a forest—dense, dark, and full of threats. People such as Dona Rosario saw it a different way: as a place that their ancestors had tended and shaped, mixing old traditions with something of their own. They had been forced to live hidden lives, always fearing that they would lose their land. Now they would be free to live in their creation, the world's richest garden.

CURRENTS OF LIFE

THE WAY I LIKE TO PUT IT, MY FAMILY IS
partly responsible for the worms. The worms
are five species that first appeared about forty
years ago in the mountain rice terraces north
of Manila, in the Philippines. By "my family," I
mean my grandfather, who in 1959 became the
headmaster of a private school near New York
City. In order to have breakfast every day with
half a dozen different students, he had asked
the school to provide him with a bigger table.
The table that arrived was made of Philippine
mahogany.

The wood it was made from is not true
mahogany, but it looks like mahogany, especially
when stained, and it may be called mahogany.
The tree was extremely common in the
Philippines. Exports soared in the 1950s. Most
of the wood went to Japan and the United States,
where it was made into furniture, decking, and

trim. A key source of mahogany was the interior of the big Philippine island of Luzon, where the former Spanish city of Manila is located. The interior of Luzon is a zone of rice terraces. For centuries people have cultivated rice on these long, skinny paddies that hug the sides of the hills, laddering up the slopes for miles in every direction. The United Nations Educational, Scientific, and Cultural Organization (UNESCO) has named Ifugao, where the terraces are highly picturesque, a World Heritage Site. Some Ifugao terraces wrap completely around hills, making the hills look like green wedding cakes fifty layers high.

When I visited Ifugao while doing research for this book, I learned that the terraces were dying. Giant earthworms from somewhere overseas had invaded them, digging huge tunnels that caused water to flow out of the paddies, killing the rice plants. Terraces that had lasted two thousand years, I was told, would disappear in a decade. The terraces had survived invasions before. In the 1980s the Philippines had imported golden apple snails from Brazil into the country's rice paddies in the hope of starting an industry of edible snails. They had done so even though the island of Taiwan, off the coast of China, had imported golden apple snails for the same reason in 1979, only to have the snails turn into a major threat to Taiwan's rice crop. Just as the hope of an edible snail industry had failed in Taiwan, it failed in the Philippines, and soon the snails were eating everything in sight. Eventually the farmers learned to control the snails. Worms remain the more important problem.

In 2008, scientists discovered nine new species of worms in the terraces. They weren't exotic invaders from another land—they had always been living in the forests of the Philippines, probably in small numbers. Yet when the slopes around Ifugao were logged for mahogany, the environment changed around the worms, and they migrated to the rice paddies. The source of the problem was not an introduced species. It was the worldwide demand for Philippine mahogany.

The problem, in short, was my grandfather. According to antiglobalization activists, his innocent wish for a new table, multiplied by ten thousand or more, set off an ecological apocalypse in which chainsaw-wielding goons flooded Luzon's mountains in their desire to tear out every tree. Left unchecked, greed would soon destroy the beautiful, age-old arrangement of terraces, wiping out traditional livelihoods with hardly a thought! It was a lesson in the evils of globalization.

Or was it? Recent research has shown that although the heart of the terraced area is as many as two thousand years old, the great bulk of the terraces are at most a few hundred years old. They were built by Filipinos who, after the Spaniards seized Manila, fled into the interior to escape Spanish demands for labor. These terraces, in other words, were largely the creation of the same great exchange that was now destroying them. In their way, they were a monument to the galleon trade, created by globalization, like the worms that were wrecking them.

Looking around Ifugao, I was struck by the number of abandoned, crumbling terraces. People were walking away from their farms. It was easy to understand. Ifugao is one of the poorer regions in the Philippines. The United Nations estimates that a typical family's land can feed them for just five months of the year. Most

(right)
The Traveller-7.

370

people actually depend on the sweet potato or buy rice at reduced prices from the government. Meanwhile, the great city Manila, throbbing with music and light, promises jobs, education, and excitement to young people. Some terrace communities now exist mainly to provide a fine backdrop to photographs.

A ray of hope came in 2005, from a plan hatched to export heirloom rice from Ifugao to the United States and Europe. It was a struggle. In order to grow enough rice to sell abroad, farmers had to band together into new organizations, master new techniques, and build new equipment. As a result, Ifugao culture is drastically changing—all for the benefit, as one scientist put it, of faraway people who want to pat themselves on the back for their enlightenment when they click the link to order fancy, expensive heirloom rice from Ifugao. The global market is not the answer, say activists, but the problem! Hooking Ifugao into the worldwide network of exchange simply makes the farmers more dependent than ever on the whims of distant consumers.

What is being lost? What would count as saving it? In a world so interconnected, there are

(*right*)
A small resort occupies the point at Maujao, where Asia, Europe, and the Americas met for the first time.

no easy answers.

On another trip I visited the town of Bulalacao, on the Philippine island of Mindoro. From there I took a boat up the coast to the place where Spain, in the form of Legazpi's men, had encountered China, in the form of two trading junks, back in 1570. It was a shallow bay, a nick in the coast with a half-built resort on one point. My guide, Rudmar, told me that the resort would be used by executives from Manila and by Filipinos who now lived and worked in other countries but wanted to vacation in a traditional setting.

Rudmar stood with his back to the water, scowling at the hills. The hills of Mindoro, like those of Luzon, had been stripped of their timber. The floods that followed deforestation had wiped out farms and villages. The government ultimately banished most logging, but the damage had been done. The floods and erosion had poured over Mindoro's beautiful beaches, permanently staining them. "They took the color from the earth," Rudmar said. He wanted his home back.

Yet there were real benefits from the logging, too. My grandfather got his table. Craftsmen got paid to build it. Shipping companies got paid to carry it, giving people jobs. Even the men with chainsaws were just putting food on their tables. In cases like this, the gains and losses are not distributed equally. The losses are intense and local, but the gains are spread around the world.

Another complication is the welter of mixed motives. People want the goods and services that the worldwide market provides. Smartphones, aerodynamic sneakers, factory-made furniture—people desire these things. If they can, they will get them, or their children will. At the same time, people want to resist change, to stand on their own ground in a place that feels uniquely like home. As billions of people march through increasingly identical landscapes, that place becomes harder to find. Things feel changed and scary. Some people hunker down into their local dialects or customary clothing or an imagined version of their own history or religion. Others enfold themselves in their homes and gardens. A few pick up weapons. Even as the world unifies, its parts split into smaller parts. Unity or division—which will win out? Or can the conflict be avoided?

Later that day, back in Bulalacao, I came upon some women and children tending a family garden around a palm-thatched home. Towering above their heads were tall stalks of corn, now the second-most important crop in the Philippines. I spent a few minutes watching the family.

Gardeners work in partnership with what nature provides. They experiment all the time, fiddling with this, trying out that. People take seeds and stick them in the ground to see what happens—that's how Ifugao villagers bred hundreds of types of rice in a few centuries. Gardens are places of constant change, but the changes are owned by the gardener, which is why gardens feel like home.

In that Bulalacao garden the Columbian Exchange had been adapted and remade. Families had taken the biological assaults of the outside world and made them into something of their own. The women were weeding around the cornstalks. Every stalk carried its American past in its DNA, but the kernels in the cobs were swelling with the next season's growth.

200,000,000 BC: Geological forces begin to
   break up the world's single giant continent,
   Pangaea, separating the hemispheres. After
   this, Eurasia and the Americas develop
   completely different sets of plants and
   animals.

AD 1096: Europeans who go to the Middle
   East during the First Crusade encounter
   sugarcane, which was first domesticated
   thousands of years earlier on the Asian
   island of New Guinea.

1405–1433: China sends huge fleets,
   commanded by an admiral named Zheng
   He, on voyages through Southeast Asia and
   as far as southern Africa.

1493: Columbus's second voyage establishes
   the first lasting European settlement in the
   Americas. It also ends the long separation of
   the hemispheres—and sets off the ecological

convulsion known as the Columbian Exchange.

1514: Only twenty-six thousand of the native Taino remain on Hispaniola, where there had probably been several hundred thousand before Europeans arrived.

1518: In the first environmental calamity of the modern era, accidentally imported African scale insects in Hispaniola lead to an explosion of fire ants. Spaniards flee the ant-infested island.

1523: Conquistador Hernán Cortés begins growing sugarcane on his estate in Mexico.

1525: China's Ming dynasty, determined to wipe out sea trade by private individuals, orders all private ships destroyed.

1526: Indians from Mexico play their traditional ball game in Spain, giving Europeans a first look at a substance entirely unknown to them: rubber.

1545: Spaniards discover the world's biggest silver strike in Bolivia. In the next century, the world's supply of this precious metal will more than double, giving Europe an economic edge that will help it colonize Africa, Asia, and the Americas.

1547: A group of the pirate-smugglers known as *wokou* begin operating near the city of Yuegang in southeastern China's Fujian province; they will eventually become leading players in one of the major economic parts of the Columbian Exchange: the trade that brings Spanish silver into China in exchange for Chinese goods such as silks and pottery.

1549: Tobacco, the addictive American drug that becomes a global craze, first appears in China.

1550–1570: A cold period called the Little Ice Age brings unusually severe weather and crop failures to the Northern Hemisphere.

1571: Miguel López de Legazpi colonizes Manila and establishes continual trade with China. Knitting the entire inhabited planet into a single web of trade, Legazpi's actions are the beginning of today's economic globalization.

1590s: The first sweet potatoes, native to the Americas, are smuggled into China from the Philippines; sweet potatoes soon become a staple crop and help fuel a population boom.

1607: The first English colonists land at what became Jamestown, Virginia.

Around 1615: Earthworms come to northern

North America in English ship ballast.
During the next three centuries, they will
reengineer forests from the Ohio Valley to
Hudson Bay.

1619: The Jamestown colonists get the first
representative government in the English
colonies and also buy the first Africans
imported as slaves.

1620: Jamestown is shipping fifty thousand
pounds of tobacco to Europe yearly—a figure
that will soon skyrocket.

1630–1660: The gush of American silver
finally causes the price of silver to collapse,
setting off the world's first global economic
calamity.

1644: China's Ming dynasty collapses.
Millions of dispossessed people pour into
the mountains, where they grow maize
and sweet potatoes, American crops first
smuggled into China from Manila and other
European bases.

1650s: The maroon state of Palmares in Brazil
covers ten thousand square miles; it will
remain independent until the 1690s.

1680–1700: The number of slaves in the
English North American colonies increases

sharply, as colonists turn to slavery rather than indentured servitude to meet their labor needs.

1698: Scottish colonists establish the short-lived settlement of New Edinburgh on the coast of Panama; it fails due to disease and poor planning.

1739: Spanish authorities establish the town of Gracia Real de Santa Teresa de Mosé in their Florida colony to house escaped slaves from the English colonies; it is the first legally recognized community of free African Americans north of Mexico.

1762: Self-governing maroons known as Bush Negroes force the Dutch colonial government of Suriname, in South America, to agree to a peace treaty.

1775: Food riots persuade King Louis XVI of France to let the pioneering nutritional chemist Antoine-Augustin Parmentier stage publicity stunts to promote potatoes from Peru. Broad stretches of northern Europe are soon covered with a monoculture of potatoes.

1781: During the Revolutionary War, Britain's "southern strategy" pushes Cornwallis's army into the malaria zone, an area dominated by malaria parasites introduced from Europe and Africa. Defeated by malaria, Cornwallis surrenders without a fight to General George Washington, ending the Revolutionary War.

1820s: Europeans and Americans begin buying a new type of waterproof shoes called galoshes, made of rubber.

1840s: Guano from South America becomes a valuable commodity once it is found to be an excellent agricultural fertilizer.

1844: Thomas Hancock in England and Charles Goodyear in the United States receive patents for their vulcanization processes, in which natural rubber is treated with sulfur to make it stable and therefore more usable.

1845: Europe's potato monoculture, unlike anything ever seen in Peru, is vulnerable to another Peruvian import: the potato blight, possibly carried to Europe in a guano shipment. Ravaging the continent from Russia to Ireland, the blight causes a famine that kills an estimated two million people, half of them in Ireland.

1856–1896: The amount of rubber that Brazil exports increases by ten times.

1861: An explosion of Colorado potato beetles, carried north from Mexico by the Columbian Exchange, ravages fields in North American and then Europe.

1876: An Englishman named Henry Wickham smuggles rubber trees out of Brazil. Afterward, the British plant rubber trees in Southeast Asia, much of which is soon covered with this foreign tree, and the Amazonian rubber boom collapses.

1880s: The rising chemical industry begins the quest for chemical pesticides to kill agricultural pests.

1880–1912: Industrializing nations, desperate for the elastic belts, pliable gaskets, and absorbent tires needed by steam engines and vehicles, buy all the rubber they can get from the Amazon's rubber trees.

1900: After several centuries of the Columbian Exchange, many cities in the tropics have lost people and importance. All the world's most populous cities except Tokyo are located in Europe or the United States.

1950s: During the Korean War, the United States bans the sale to China of natural rubber, which has many military uses.

1960s: The government of Brazil builds highways across the interior to open up the northern part of the country to settlement by migrants from central and southern Brazil.

1963: A successful effort to increase food production in the Chinese village of Dazhai sparks a wave of agricultural reform, which results in deforestation and increased flooding.

1979: The golden apple snail is sent from Brazil to Taiwan to launch an edible snail industry there. It escapes, multiplies, and becomes a major menace to the island's rice crop. In spite of this problem, the snail is later imported into the Philippines.

1981: A new form of potato blight, originating in Mexico, is detected in Europe. In China, in the hope of halting deforestation, the government begins requiring citizens to plant trees every year.

1988: Brazil's new democratic constitution gives the residents of *quilombos* legal ownership of the land these settlements occupy.

1990s: China begins investing in rubber plantations in neighboring Southeast Asian nations.

1991: The Columbus Lighthouse, a memorial to
 Columbus, is completed in the Dominican
 Republic after long delays and amid some
 controversy.

2008: Scientists discover that worms from the
 forests of the Philippines have migrated into
 rice paddies because logging of wood for the
 export market changed their natural habitat.

2009: Potato blight wipes out many potatoes
 and tomatoes on the East Coast of the
 United States. Also, based on new studies of
 historical records, researchers estimate the
 number of Africans brought to the Americas
 as slaves between 1500 and 1840 to be 11.7
 million.

ABOLISH To end or do away with; the act of
   abolishing something is called abolition, as
   in the abolition of slavery
ANTHROPOLOGY The study of human beings;
   various branches of anthropology focus on
   human origins, on the biological and social
   features of human populations, on people's
   relationships with their environments
   and societies, on family life, and on the
   differences and similarities among cultures
ARCHAEOLOGY The study of past human
   cultures through their remains, such as
   fossils, skeletons, buildings, and objects that
   people made and used
BOTANY The branch of the life sciences that
   focuses on plants
CAPITAL In finance, wealth (in the form of
   money or other property with value) that has

been invested or is available to be invested in a business or in financial investments such as stocks

CHATTEL SLAVERY A form of slavery in which enslaved people are regarded as property and have few or no rights

CHINO An Asian immigrant or person of Asian descent in Spain's Mexico colony

COLONIZE To settle in or claim a new territory and establish political control over it

COLUMBIAN EXCHANGE The transfer of people, plants, animals, diseases, money, and cultural practices among the continents that began when Christopher Columbus's voyages permanently connected Eurasia and the Americas

COMMODITY MONEY Money made out of a commodity, or something that has value in itself, such as silver coins; whatever the denomination of a silver coin, silver is worth something purely as a metal

CONQUISTADOR One of the Spanish conquerors of Indian states in the Americas in the sixteenth and seventeenth centuries

CURRENCY Whatever the people in a given country or region agree to use as money; currency can take the form of paper bills, metal coins, or other objects such as furs or shells

DENOMINATION The "face value" of a piece of money, usually stamped or printed on a coin or bill

DNA Short for deoxyribonucleic acid; the set of molecules that contain the genetic code for every living thing and are the basis for genetic traits passed from parents to their offspring; DNA is made up of genes grouped into strands called chromosomes

DOMESTIC, DOMESTICATED Not wild; the versions of plants or animals that people farm, herd, or otherwise use on a regular basis

ECOLOGICAL Having to do with the relationships among living things and their environments; the study of those relationships is called ecology

ECOLOGICAL RELEASE The sudden arrival of a species in a new territory where it has not existed before and where it has few or no natural enemies; ecological release usually results in a population explosion of the new species

ECONOMICS The study of how people use scarce resources to achieve their goals; often an analysis of markets and wealth

ENDEMIC Existing in a certain place or area;
a disease is considered endemic when it
commonly occurs among people in a given area

EPIDEMIC A severe outbreak of disease that
affects far more people than normal

EURASIA The large land mass that contains
Europe and Asia

FAMINE A severe, often prolonged shortage of
food across an entire region or country, with
serious health effects

FERAL Living in a wild state; plants, animals,
gardens, or whole ecosystems that were once
domesticated become feral if they or their
descendants no longer live under human
control

FERTILIZER Something added to soil to
provide needed or extra nutrition to plants;
fertilizers range from manure, ashes,
and leaves to chemical mixtures made in
laboratories and factories

FIAT MONEY Money that has value only because
it is backed by a government, bank, or
corporation; dollar bills, which have no value
in themselves as paper objects, are examples
of fiat money

GALLEON A large sailing ship developed in

Europe in the sixteenth century, used as
both a warship and for carrying cargo; the
biggest galleons were cargo vessels for long-
distance trade

GENETICS The branch of biology concerned with
the ways DNA causes variety and heredity in
living things

GENUS A group of closely related species

GLOBALIZATION The process by which the
various parts of the world have become
increasingly interconnected through the
exchange of species, through shared
economic and communications networks,
and through the movements of people

GUANO The dried waste of birds built up in
deposits over years

HEMISPHERE One half of the world; the
Northern Hemisphere contains Europe,
much of Asia, and North America; the
Southern Hemisphere contains Africa,
some of Asia, Australia, and South
America; the Eastern Hemisphere contains
Europe, Asia, Africa, and Australia; and
the Western Hemisphere contains the
Americas

IMMIGRANT Someone who enters a new

country or region to live after leaving his or
her homeland

IMPERIAL Having to do with an empire or
empire-like state

IMPERIALISM Empire building; extending
a country's power in the world, whether
through diplomacy or war

INDENTURED SERVANT Someone who works
under an indenture, a contract that binds
the worker for a set period of time; many
people came to the American colonies
as indentured servants, accepting the
indenture in return for the price of their
passage to America

INDIGENOUS Native to a place

INFLATION In economics, inflation is a general
increase in the cost of goods and services;
because things cost more, the purchasing power
of each individual unit of money goes down

LAZY-BED FARMING A traditional agricultural
practice in which farmers dig the sod from
their fields, pile it upside down into ridges
separated by furrows or open spaces, and plant
their crops in the exposed soil of the ridges

LOESS A type of earth that is made up of packed
silt; it can be deposited by wind or carried

away by flowing water

MAROON An escaped or fugitive slave, or the
free-living descendant of escaped slaves

MICROORGANISM A living thing, such as a
bacterium or virus, that is so small it can be
seen only through a microscope

MIGRANT Someone who leaves his or her
homeland to live in a new country

MONOPOLY In economics, the sole control of a
resource, service, or commodity that has value

MORAL Having to do with morality or ethics,
which is the consideration of what is good
and bad, or right and wrong, behavior

PADDY A field that can be flooded with shallow
water for growing rice

PALEOCLIMATOLOGY The study of climate in
earlier eras of human or geological history

PESTICIDE Something used to kill a pest;
specific types of pesticides include
herbicides for weeds, insecticides for insects,
and fungicides for fungus

PRIVATEER A sea captain who has permission
from his government to attack and loot the
ships and settlements of nations at war with
his government, in a kind of legal piracy

QUARANTINE The isolation of a person or

people believed to have a contagious illness,
or the prevention of them from entering a
city or country

QUILOMBO A community of escaped or fugitive
African slaves and Indians in Brazil; now a
community inhabited by the descendants of
the fugitives

QUOTA A set amount or percentage; a target to
be met

SILT Particles of earth that are smaller and finer
than sand; sometimes called "stone dust"

TERRACE A flat surface constructed on a slope
or hillside by making a wall across the
slope and filling the space behind it with
earth; hillsides can be covered with rows of
terraces, each rising from the one below it,
like stair steps

TOXIC Poisonous or severely harmful

TUBER The edible root of a plant, such as a
potato or sweet potato

WOKOU The Chinese term for "Japanese pirate,"
although most wokou were not Japanese,
and many were smugglers rather than
pirates

Maps by Nick Springer and Tracy Pollock, Springer Cartographics LLC. Sources as follows:

21, Redrawn from Guitar 1998:13

66, Base map by Nick Springer published in *National Geographic*, May 2007; data from Helen Rountree, Martin D. Gallivan; additional data from Barlow 2003:22. My thanks to William McNulty and the rest of the *NG* cartography staff for allowing Nick and me to adapt these maps.

96, Data from Preservation Virginia, Wetlands Vision (UK), Smith 1956. My thanks to Robert C. Anderson and William Thorndale for critiques and suggestions.

122, Data from Kiszewski et al. 2004:488; Webb 2009:87; Gilmore 1955:348; author's interview, Donald Gaines.

191 (bottom), Redrawn from Central Bureau of Meteorological Sciences (China) 1981.

237, Redrawn from Bourke 1694:806.

299, Base map redrawn from Galloway 1977:178; additional data from Disney 2009, Ouerfelli 2008, Vieira 1992.

308, Redrawn from Barrett, 1970:8.

351, Data from Price 2011:6–7 (Suriname, Guyane); Tardieu 2009 (Panama); La Rosa Corso 2003 (Cuba); Lane 2002:chap. 1 (Esmeraldas); Perez 2000:618 (Venezuela); Landers 1999:236 (Florida); Reis and Gomes eds. 1996 (Brazil); Aptheker 1996 (US); Friedemann 1993:70–71 (Colombia); Deive 1989:73 (Hispaniola); Carroll 1977 (Mexico); author's interviews, Fundação Cultural Palmares and Instituto de Terras do Pará.

AUTHOR

4; 13–14; 30 (top); 34; 124, E. Riou, *La Guyane Française*, 1867; 144 (top), Author's collection, 1764 gazetteer; 144 (bottom); 170–1, 172 (bottom); 180; 192; 201; 203; 254; 260, Author's collection (Iles, *Leading American Investors*, 1912); 264, Author's Collection (Hancock, *Personal Narrative of the Origin and Progress of the Caoutchouc*, 1857); 273 (bottom), Author's collection, (Falcão, *Album do Acre*, 1906–07); 284–5; 286; 338; 352; 354–55, chart and photograph by author; 357; 363; 371; 373

LIBRARY OF CONGRESS

ii; 208, Russell Lee; 26–27, L. Prang & Co.; 56, Lewis Wickes Hine; 79–81, G3880 1667.F3; 127, LC-USZ62-95078; 133, LCUSZC4-9408; 244, Library of Congress, Prints & Photographs Division, FSA/OWI Collection, [LC-USW33- 043088-ZC]

VARIOUS ILLUSTRATIONS

1, Flickr/Kristen Cronin; 4, Flickr/Ginger Warden; 51, Copyright © Tomás Filsinger, 2009; 52–53, 71, and 75, Virtual Jamestown, Permission by Randy Shifflett 64, Courtesy of Crawford Lake Conservation Area, Conservation Halton (Ontario); 75, (bottom), 1834.1, badge, ca. 1660; 89, Lennart Nilsson/SCANPIX; 152, Courtesy Bob Reis (anythinganywhere.com); 134–5, China Photos/Getty Images; 156 (top), Fundación Cultural Banco Central de Bolivia, Potosí; 156 (bottom), f US 2257.50* Houghton Library, Harvard University (Theodo de Bry, *Collectiones peregrinationum*, 1590); 161 (bottom), Courtesy Ken and Sue Goodreau, New World Treasures; 200, Courtesy Town of Gaoxigou, Shaanxi; 213, Dept. of Rare Books and manuscripts, Royal Library, Copenhagen (Felipe Guaman Poma de Ayala, El Primer Nueva Corónica y Buen Gobierno [GKS 2234-4[o]); 215, 219–20, International Potato Center (Peru); 224 and 227, Courtesy New York Public Library (Alexander Gardner, *Rays of Sunlight from South American*, 1865); 232 and 234, Courtesy "Views of Famine," http://adminstaff.vassar.edu/sttaylor/FAMINE/ (*Illustrated News*); 239, Copyright © National Museums Northern Ireland 2010, Collection Ulster Museum, Belfast (Courtesy of the Trustees of national Museums Northern Ireland); 242, Courtesy Clark Erickson; 249, Courtesy Homer Babbidge Library, University of Connecticut; 257 (top), Germanisches Nationalmuseum (Christoph Weiditz, *Trachenbuch*, 1529); 270, Courtesy Yale University Library; 278, Courtesy John Loadman (www.bouncing-balls.com); 281, Flickr Commons, *India Book World*, 1899; 290–1 and 317 (bottom), Collection of Malú and Alejandra Excandón, Mexico City; 299, Courtesy Huntington Library (Jan van de Straet, *Nova Reporta*, 1584); 305–7 and 313, Courtesy Casa Nacional de Moneda, Potosí; 311, Copyright © 2010 Alvy Ray Smith (www.alvyray.com), freely usable under a Creative Commons attribution-NoDerivs 3.0 Unported License. Data from Thomas 1995:626–27, Hemming 1993:488–95, Muñoz de San Pedro 1951. My thanks to Matthew Restall for advice and to Alvy Ray Smith for his generosity and enthusiasm; 316 (top), Denver Art Museum, Collection of Jan and Frederick Mayer; 316 (bottom) and 317 (top), Private collection, Spain; 320, Courtesy Biblioteca Nacional de España (Durán, *Historia de las Indias de Nueva España*, 1587); 326, Basílica de Nuestra Señora de la Merced (Buenos Aires); 331, Flickr, Felipe Miguel; 333, Flickr, Avener Prado / FESTCINEAMAZONIA; 341, Courtesy New York Public Library (Chapin, "Col. Taylor at the battle of Okey Chobey," 1861

WELLCOME IMAGES

84, Wellcome Library, London. Wellcome Images images@wellcome.ac.uk http://wellcomeimages.org Postcard: mosquito net to be worn as a veil. early 20th century; 94 and 128–29, Wellcome Library, London, *The Journal of Hygiene*, Cambridge University Press, Cambridge, 1901; 104, Wellcome Images (V0010519); 161 (top), Wellcome Library, London, A llama standing on a rock. Colored wood engraving by J. W. Whimper; 168, Science Museum, Wellcome Library, London; 179, Wellcome Library no. 40446i, A silkworm (Phaloena mori) shown as imago, larva, pupa and egg. Etching by M. Griffith; 325, Wellcome Library, V0043803

38 (bottom); 62, Courtesy Virtual Jamestown (detail, John Smith, *Map of Virgina*); 103, James Gathany Content Providers: CDC; 172 (top), Stefan Teodosic; 187–9, Huang Zi (17th century); 204–5, קוביקמ ורוא איגש י"ע סלוצ דעס; 237, I.Sáček, senior; 257 (bottom), Daderot; 267–8, Wales Goodyear Rubbers, 1891; 296–7, U.S. Navy photo by Mass Communication Specialist 2nd Class Kim Williams, image released by the United States Navy with the ID 100219-N-9643W-340; 346, Roberto Sabino